The Spiritual Architecture of a Soul

Memories of a Warrior, a Guardian, and the Ancient Path Home.

By Javier Lora

THE LATTICEWORK PRESS *Hesperia, California*

Copyright

The Spiritual Architecture of a Soul *Memories of a Warrior, a Guardian, and the Ancient Path Home.*

ISBN: 979-8-234-06291-8

Published by:

THE LATTICEWORK PRESS

Cover Design by:

Javier Lora

Edited by:

Javier Lora

Disclaimer

This book is a memoir. It reflects the author's present recollections of experiences over a lifetime. Some names and identifying details have been changed to protect the privacy of individuals. The spiritual and philosophical views expressed are those of the author and are intended for inspirational and educational purposes.

Printed in the United States of America

First Edition: 2026

DEDICATION

To My Lineage: The Living Blueprint

To my wife, my children, and my grandchildren—the Ancient Companions who have returned to walk this segment of the journey with me:

I have written these words so that you may understand the invisible structure of the world we shared. In our home, you knew me as a father and a provider, but I have also been your sentry. I have spent this lifetime standing guard over the frequency of our family, ensuring that the vessel we built together was strong enough to hold the light of your souls.

This book is my final gift to you—a map of the spiritual architecture that has guided my every step.

To my children, Kori and Kevin: You are not merely my descendants; you are the architects of your own milestones. I hope these memories help you recognize the "Dual Vision» within yourselves and give you the courage to follow your own "Yellow Lights".

To my second daughter, Samantha: Whose transition taught me the true meaning of grace. Thank you for the rhythm of your thoughts, which still reaches me, and for proving that the bond of the soul is never severed.

To my grandchildren, Olivia, Kye, Ava, and Natalia: You are the newest growth on our ancient tree—seasoned spirits who have returned to gather a harvest of wisdom generations in the making. Know that the foundation beneath your feet is unshakable.

To my wife, Karen: You are the grounding force that made this architecture possible. Without your clarity, the sentry's watch would not have endured.

When the time comes for my physical watch to end, do not look for me in the past. Look for me in the Latticework. I will be there—in the living architecture of your lives, in the quiet protection that surrounds you, and in the absolute, warm peace of our shared home.

The blueprint is complete.
The architecture holds.
Carry the light forward.

TABLE OF CONTENTS

INTRODUCTION

The Sentry's Briefing

Most people spend their lives believing that the world is a collection of random events—a series of coincidences tied together by biological necessity and the pursuit of comfort. I am here to tell you that this is an illusion.

For as long as I can remember, I have seen a different reality. I have lived with a "Dual Vision": one eye fixed on the physical world of heavy machinery, hazardous waste, and the tangible demands of a career; the other eye fixed on a shimmering, multidimensional architecture that connects every soul, every event, and every lifetime. I call this structure the Latticework.

This book is not a traditional memoir. It is a debriefing. It is the record of a soul who arrived here with a specific contract: to serve as a Sentry. Through the chapters that follow, I will share with you *The Spiritual Architecture of a Soul*—a map of the memories I have gathered as a Warrior, a Guardian, and a traveler on the Ancient Path Home.

Throughout these pages, you will walk with me through the "Fire" of my early childhood and the "Warrior's Penance" of my youth. You will see the aqua-green lights of the desert sky and hear the silent instructions of the Guardians who have mentored me from the unseen. You will witness the "Sacred Commitment" I made to my family—a vow that transcended the boundaries of life and death.

I am sharing this blueprint with you now because we are all, in our own way, site managers for a spiritual construction project. We are all "Ancient Companions" who agreed to meet here, in this density, to learn the most profound lesson the universe has to offer: the value of human feeling.

As you read, I invite you to look for your own "Yellow Lights"—those intuitive warnings that guide your path. I invite you to recognize the "Ancient

Echoes" in the eyes of your children and the "Necessary Friction" in the lives of your kin.

The scaffolding of your life may feel heavy, and the journey may at times feel fragmented, but I assure you: there is a design. From the "Final Vista" where I now stand, the view is clear. The architecture holds.

Welcome to the Latticework.

CHAPTER I

The Awakening of Memory

Early recollections and the first glimpses of the unseen

My earliest vivid memories are from 1960s Mexico City, starting when I was just two years old. Even at that age, I possessed a mature and familiar understanding of my family's activities and conversations. I was always puzzled by why they spoke to me as if I didn't comprehend them; I knew this was only temporary, requiring nothing more than patience.

As a child, I had a powerful ability to listen and perceive, instinctively reading energy, expressions, and body language. Deciphering this secret language gave me a profound sense of purpose—a constant internal compass that has pointed my way ever since.

It was a feeling amplified and enriched by my dreams, which were often less like fiction and more like memories.

My vivid dreams have always been a source of inspiration and a personal time machine. In these early dreams, I traveled through countless historical timelines, experiencing lives as a child, a teenager, and an adult. I endured everything from adversity, loss, and death to contentment, success, and war. I didn't just witness these lives—I felt them. The emotions were so real that they would often linger for days after I woke.

These dreams were often followed by visions of silhouetted figures who, through a cascade of jumbled words, revealed the reason and meaning behind my experiences. To me, this was proof that these were my past lives.

My first and most frequent dream begins with me in a large chair, surrounded by the silhouettes of people I know—yet they are strangers. Their words are a torrent of demands, advice, and expectations, a confusing jumble of noise. But I am not overwhelmed; instead of a chaotic mess, I hear each voice and thought with perfect clarity. It is in that moment, amidst the din, that I finally understand what everyone is saying and, more importantly, what I have agreed to accomplish.

I am then violently thrust through a sudden distance, collapsing into the warm, confined space of a fetus. The abrupt abandonment and utter solitude leave me feeling lost, but that uncertainty becomes my anchor. It doesn't weaken me; it reinforces my resolve to embrace the challenges of this unknown world.

Since my earliest days, my dreams have been of battle. I have led armies to conquer new lands in 320 BC, feeling the desert heat of the Mediterranean; I have fought as a Native American warrior and taken part in the Revolutionary, Civil, and Second World Wars. Whether it was hand-to-hand combat with sword and shield or modern warfare with knives and guns, the strain, the sounds, the wounds, and the death were all unforgettable.

In both my dreams and waking life, I was visited by guides who reminded me that I had a purpose to achieve. While I did not yet know what that purpose was, their constant presence made me fully aware that they were my protectors. This guidance continued throughout every phase of my life, strengthening my scientific knowledge and intuition after each experience. This intuition was immediately evident in my connection to the non-human world.

From a young age, I felt a deep connection to animals, sensing their emotions and knowing they could feel mine. This bond was especially strong with dogs, and it became a powerful part of my life. In 1960s Mexico City, stray dogs were a constant presence. My parents and neighbors often cautioned me to stay inside to avoid their bites, but as a small child, I found them comforting. I even believed the dogcatcher to be a hero—perhaps because I sensed the strays' suffering and thought he was helping, or simply because the adults around me said he was.

At just three and four years old, I would sit on the sidewalk, watching the world go by. The dogs would instinctively seek me out, lying down to rest beside me. I felt a sense of comfort and protection in these peaceful moments, which only ended when a panicked adult spotted four or five dogs at my side, or when the distant sound of dogs barking from a dogcatcher's truck sent the strays scattering.

While I instinctively found solace and trust in the nonverbal world of animals, the realm of human relationships soon proved far more complex—and stinging.

My mother managed our household with the support of our extended family while my father was in the United States, working to prepare the way for us. In his absence, I spent more time than ever with aunts, uncles, cousins, and grandparents. I was quickly exposed to their criticism, arrogance, and harsh treatment, sensing a profound lack of sincerity toward my parents. I felt the sting of it all, and the experience immediately eroded my trust.

Despite this, I began to understand our family and national culture; however, I also sensed their expectations, which made me feel wary and distant. This intuition was only reinforced by my dreams. I had recurring visions of betrayal by those I trusted most—betrayals that, in several past lifetimes, had led to my death.

Seeking refuge from these human complexities, I found a different kind of belonging in the land itself. A profound sense of patriotism took hold—not for the people, but for the soil. This allegiance became a sanctuary untainted by personal conflict, a foundational feeling that would shape the rest of my journey.

My mother, however, was my singular, unwavering constant—the one person in whom my eroded trust could still find a foundation. As the youngest of six children, I was always at her side, accompanying her everywhere she went. My closest sibling was four years older than me, so at three years old, I would make the long walk to the open market with her.

What I loved most about those trips was the vibrant chaos, especially the sight of the livestock for sale. One day, while we were at a vegetable stand and my mother was being attended to, I noticed a vendor behind me with a cage of chickens and a separate box of downy chicks. I walked up to see the chicks; the vendor smiled and asked if I wanted one. "Yes," I said, "but I need to ask my mother."

When I turned back, my mother was no longer there. I searched the market for her for what seemed like forever. I ended up at the market's edge, watching the endless stream of people. A sudden, chilling dread washed over me: I was alone.

Suddenly, from the surrounding crowd, a man stood at my side. "You must go home now," he instructed, his voice imbued with a calm certainty. My gaze fell to his worn, tattered pants; before I could look up to see his face, he pressed on: "Let's go, your mother is worried." He walked beside me, always to my right, methodically pointing out every intersection, naming streets, and counting down the blocks—a constant, unwavering reminder of our path.

The strangest part was the sheer lack of acknowledgment from the crowd. People would normally engage with a small child, yet these passersby merely looked through us—an unnerving experience. We finally reached my block. He guided me across the street, and the moment my foot touched the curb, I turned to offer my thanks.

He was simply gone. The pavement behind me was deserted.

As I rounded the corner, my uncles, cousins, and brothers came into view, preparing their search party in front of my grandmother's house. "There he is!" my uncle shouted. A wave of relief broke over them as they surged forward. In the center was my mother—her face a study in pure panic, instantly replaced by profound relief.

My first encounter with death occurred when I was three, following a fiery bus accident that claimed my aunt's life. In our country, it was customary to hold the wake at home. The viewing was held in my grandmother's living room at the front of the house, entered through a covered carport.

The casket sat in the center of the room, surrounded by chairs. My mother told us children we could go inside once the adults had left. Throughout the day, I played in the carport, watching family and friends grieve. As night fell and people began to leave, my mother stood with me in the far corner of the carport. The living room door was open, and I could see several relatives sitting and sobbing.

Suddenly, I saw my deceased aunt walking along the perimeter of the room. She was looking down at the sobbing relatives, but as she reached the last chair near the door, she looked out into the carport. Her eyes scanned the space and made direct eye contact with me. Her face showed an expression of surprise, followed by a soft smile when she realized I was looking right at her. She slowly turned and walked back into the room.

Confused, I asked my mother again why everyone was crying, and she explained what death was. I told her I had just seen my aunt and asked when we could go in to see her. When we finally entered, my mother was holding me. The casket was open in the center of the room, but my aunt's face was covered by her wedding dress and veil.

I wanted to see her face, but my mother explained it was covered because of her injuries. I insisted my aunt wasn't burned—that she was whole—and that I had just seen her. My mother looked at me with a surprised expression, but she didn't say a word.

These experiences—the inexplicable visions and the unnerving mysteries—were simply the fabric of my earliest childhood. Our home stood near the airport. In the summer of 1962, when I was just three, my mother suddenly woke me from my nap. Her voice was filled with almost breathless excitement as she scooped me into her arms. "You must come see President Kennedy!" she exclaimed.

As she ran toward the street, she explained he was on his way to the airport to return to the United States. The roar of the crowd grew louder as we neared the entrance—a wave of cheers and clapping. The street was a solid wall of people. My mother lifted me onto her shoulders and pointed to the left. "Look, there he is!" she said.

I turned and saw the open limousine inching slowly toward the street corner. The First Lady was on the left, with President Kennedy on the right, both waving to the roaring crowds. It was a scorching day, and what struck me most was the bright sunlight glinting powerfully off his reddish blond hair. It was a profound moment, seeing real Americans for the first time.

Then a strange silence fell. The crowd's cheering vanished, though I could still see people applauding and following the car. I wondered why I couldn't hear them. As the limousine rounded the corner, a voice clearly and distinctly spoke to me: "You will remember this. This will be important to you later."

This audible pronouncement was one manifestation of a consistent inner dialogue I came to know as guardian communication—a connection that was often both audible and intuitive. While directions and warnings surfaced in the background, the essential message was conveyed through feeling: the profound acceptance that followed guidance meant for my well-being, or the immediate sense of consequence when a warning was ignored.

With time, the process simplified further. I learned that to ask a question or seek clarity, I only needed to think it, and the response would arrive instantly.

The high-energy presence I sensed in those early years, like the voice during the motorcade, became a vivid memory that continued to manifest throughout my life. Even at five years old, I felt a deep drive to protect my family. I spent endless, solitary hours thinking and listening inwardly, content in the certainty that I was protected and never truly alone.

When my mother, my second-oldest sister, and I were the first to join my father in the United States, I embarked on that journey with great enthusiasm. I was fueled by the conviction that life would be better for all of us and that moving forward would bring me closer to whatever it was I had agreed to accomplish.

CHAPTER II

The Fire and the Fragmented Path

The formative trauma of the house fire and the lessons of early survival

In June of 1964, we finally arrived in Los Angeles. During the long trip to the United States, I had struggled to remember my father; the two years he was away, visiting us only at Christmas, had felt like an eternity. Seeing him for the first time, I saw a man concerned for his family—a proud man, driven and focused on bringing the rest of my siblings together again. That first day felt strange; I felt as if I knew him from a past life and understood what our relationship would be on this journey. From that moment, I developed a respect for him that would last his entire life.

As we drove toward our second-story apartment, I peered out the window, mesmerized by the scenery. The streets, colors, homes, and people were distinctly different yet surprisingly familiar. All the while, my sister and I listened as our father meticulously detailed our new situation and plans for our mother. Although that neighborhood is now a predominantly Latino community, back in 1964 it was Jewish, and hardly anyone spoke Spanish.

As I witnessed the challenges of the language barrier, I realized I was understanding the conversations around me. I didn't dare speak up, afraid of making a mistake, but over time it became undeniable that I understood exactly what was being said.

Soon after, our first trip to the supermarket was an amazing, eye-opening experience. The stark contrast hit me immediately: in Mexico, we had to conserve food at every meal, knowing nothing could be wasted. Too often we went to bed hungry, and many times we watched our parents sacrifice their own meals so we could eat. Now, seeing this abundance, I realized our struggle was over. I couldn't wait for my other siblings to arrive so we could all finally be together again.

Anticipation and a profound uneasiness marked the start of a new endeavor: my first day of school. My sister, eleven, and I, just five, were about to step into this unfamiliar world. For weeks, my father had cautioned me to behave and avoid trouble, knowing my active, impatient nature and my tendency to get into things. On that crucial first morning, my sister walked me to my classroom and reminded me to go straight home afterward.

As I watched her leave for her own class, a chilling realization hit me: I was alone. A cold feeling of abandonment washed over me, and I was just starting to cry when a sudden, steel-like resolve took hold.

I realized I had to do this on my own; I would have to do everything on my own from now on. That initial fear did not last; instead, it swiftly morphed into a bedrock of confidence and motivation—a feeling I would actively seek at the start of every new endeavor for the rest of my life.

Stepping into the classroom, a quiet, self-driven resolve guided my observation of the American children. Despite my inability to speak or communicate in English, I understood their jokes, their criticisms, and the teacher's attempts to correct them. This clarity only intensified during those first several months. Instead of harboring anger or hurt, I began to develop compassion for them; I was frequently reminded that I had been through far worse, and they were only children.

This feeling—of thinking as an adult and understanding that this challenging process was necessary—was a strange but comforting constant throughout my youth. Past life dreams intensified, saturated with the trauma of prejudice, slavery, imprisonment, and execution. The despair and profound sense of injustice from those lives remained deeply embedded in my soul, serving as a stark measure against how minor and petty my current difficulties felt.

As the new kid on the block, two brothers who lived down the street would periodically come over to play—one my age, the other three years older. We had a unique way of communicating: they spoke to me in English and I replied in Spanish, yet we understood each other perfectly. However, I genuinely did not care for the older boy.

Behind our apartment, the owners kept an old, off-limits garage. While the younger boy and I were playing one afternoon, the older brother suddenly yelled, "Hey! Come here, the door is open!"

We slipped into the garage. All three sections were crammed from floor to ceiling with boxes and old furniture. As we reached the final section, I saw the older boy folding a paper airplane. Before I could question him, he struck a match and lit the paper. I was at the far end of the room while they stood near the doorway. He threw the flaming airplane. It landed on a towering stack of paper, which instantly ignited, completely blocking my exit. I watched them sprint out as the flames raced up the wall and hit the ceiling, realizing with a jolt that I was trapped.

Suddenly, my gaze snapped left, catching a gleam of light between two enormous boxes. A small hole pierced the wall, and a voice—urgent and sharp—commanded:

“Get out now!”

As if shoved, I launched myself at the boxes. The hole was barely wider than my waist, but I didn't slow down. I smashed through it, ripping the opening to three times its original size, and didn't feel a thing. Scrambling free, I caught a final glimpse of the two brothers rounding the corner and disappearing.

The garage burned completely to the ground. As firemen questioned me through an interpreter, I answered their questions before she could even finish translating, which clearly made her uneasy. Once I relayed the events, the firemen knew exactly who the boy was—it was not their first time dealing with him. Despite the fact that I was the victim, I still had to face my father's punishment for being in the off-limits garage.

That unsettling experience confirmed my facility with the new language; I was speaking English fluently in no time. Reading and writing followed so quickly it felt like an overnight transformation, yet it was all strangely familiar. I loved hearing the surprised comments from my teachers, who often asked me to read to the class.

My interactions with classmates and teachers were always a strange, dual experience. While I spoke, my mind directed me to analyze everything: their eye contact, facial expressions, body language, and, most importantly, their energy and sincerity. This feeling of witnessing everything from a third-person perspective gave me the confidence to trust the process, knowing I was never truly alone.

It was also during this time that I began to sense an energy presence—a feeling that stayed with me on my walk home from school and while waiting alone for my sister. While the feeling was mostly positive, it would occasionally turn negative enough to give me chills. I soon realized that all I had to do was simply ask the negative presence to leave. At this early stage, I didn't yet grasp the full magnitude of these experiences, but I would come to understand their profound importance much later in life.

The day our entire family was reunited in the United States finally arrived. I was thrilled to welcome my older siblings and embrace this new life together, but my role quickly changed. Having arrived earlier, I—the youngest—was now the one helping them, answering endless questions about the English language and our new world.

Seeing them endure the same challenging endeavors of school and cultural adjustment that my sister and I had faced, I realized they had their own unique battles ahead. I found quiet satisfaction in this new role, knowing I simply needed to continue on my own established path.

Witnessing our family's struggles during those initial years, coupled with their constant stories of our life in Mexico—stories that often felt like echoes of the dreams I had already lived—powerfully reinforced my existing beliefs. During this time, the underlying meaning of the intense past life dreams I'd been having began to clarify. While those vivid dreams continued, their focus sharpened, becoming more detailed about my relationship interactions and the people in my life.

Soon after, a new kind of dream began: premonitions of the future. These visions would stop me cold whenever I recognized an unfolding event exactly as I had seen it. These predictive dreams intensified later in my youth and went on to profoundly shape the rest of my life.

Witnessing the turbulence of the era—the fierce anti-war protests, the urgency of the civil rights movement, the social friction between generations, and the staggering loss of President Kennedy—somehow felt uncannily familiar.

Yet one day remains clearer than all the turmoil: seeing the First Lady and the President in Mexico. That moment filled me with a powerful, unmistakable surge of American patriotism—a simple, quiet knowledge that I belonged here. After four years, the unrelenting rhythm of life in our apartment, and the unsettling shifts on our once-familiar streets, finally persuaded our father to move us to a better environment: a new home.

These foundational years in the United States were wonderful, establishing a strong motivation that would guide my future. The music, events, and people of the time provided me with a complete understanding of the culture and the specific challenges I would encounter on my path. It was a journey I felt deeply prepared to undertake.

CHAPTER III

The Warrior's Penance

Football, discipline, and the physical manifestations of the protective instinct

In 1968, our family settled into a spacious house in a town that was overwhelmingly White. Right across the street, two neighbors—a couple and a kind older gentleman who lived with his elderly mother—welcomed us with notable curiosity, pointing out that we were the first Latino family ever to live on the block.

The gentleman showed me genuine kindness, and soon, in a quiet, sympathetic tone, he began to outline the community's prejudices toward other ethnic groups. While I appreciated his sincerity, I knew deep down that whatever lay ahead couldn't be worse than what I had already faced in the past. I thanked him warmly for his concern but kept the conversation to myself.

However, it didn't take long for the gentleman's warning to be proven true. We soon overheard bitter racist comments made by the neighbors next door as they were moving out.

Public school felt like a breath of fresh air. I instantly loved the freedom of not wearing uniforms, and the other kids played with a wonderful, unreserved energy—it was a welcome change. Making friends was never an issue; I loved to run and play all sports.

However, the innocence of friendship was constantly undercut by prejudice. My new friends often repeated the things their parents said at home about "a Latino going to their school." This subtle hostility escalated when teachers began openly asking why we had moved to town, or even threatened to "send me back where I came from" if I misbehaved. These actions gave older kids more license to target me. Because my parents constantly warned me not to cause problems, I endured the harassment without reacting.

Beyond one friend who lived down the street, it wasn't until sixth grade that I was allowed to step inside the homes of my classmates. Even then, the prejudice was palpable: parents would softly tell their children, “We don't want Mexicans in this house,” or insist I could only play outside. To hear these adults—these guardians—call me a “pepper belly,” “beaner,” or “wetback” was painful. Yet my own guides would tell me:

"You will show them. They will eat their words."

I quickly realized their cruelty stemmed from profound ignorance, and in spite of everything, I couldn't help but feel sorry for them.

One by one, the family landscape began to shift. My oldest brother decided to move back to Mexico, while my second brother quickly married and started his own family, moving out shortly thereafter. Our second-oldest sister also married and moved on. Soon, only my oldest sister, my youngest sister, and I remained in the house. We watched as our older siblings stepped into their new lives while we stayed behind with our parents, maintaining the foundation of our home.

My siblings and I were raised Catholic, and my devoted mother insisted we attend church with her regularly. My father, who held a different view of organized religion, seldom accompanied us. I understood both positions, but I often made it known that I leaned toward my father’s belief: that God would hear you praying anytime, anywhere—not just in a church.

Despite my father’s strong opinions, my mother initially enrolled me in a Catholic school. It wasn't long before I became the target of a nun's discipline. I was repeatedly singled out, facing the savage crack of a heavy, round stick across the back of my legs. Every misstep or hesitation earned the stick, and I felt the full weight of the institution's hostility.

Yet the physical abuse failed to corrupt my spiritual perspective. My inner guides stepped in, their voices calm and absolute:

"Priests and nuns are just fallible people. They are meant only to support others—nothing more."

Ultimately, the sight of the bruises on my legs was proof enough for my mother. She immediately pulled me out and enrolled me in public school.

As the youngest, I grew up with a noticeable distance from my father that my older siblings didn't share. Both parents worked long hours to sustain us: my father was a highly respected Maestro (master tailor), and my mother served as the dedicated finisher in his trade. Because of my age, my father soon became concerned that living in the United States would cause me to forget my Mexican roots.

To counter this, he took me back to Mexico in 1971. We traveled during Christmas, visiting family and friends and exploring the country—a journey designed entirely for my benefit. This trip created my most indelible memories of him. I accepted the distance that had developed in our relationship because I finally understood the man: his tough upbringing and the enormous, self-imposed responsibility he carried for his family.

As he shared stories of his youth, I learned that as a child he had been forced to work to support his own siblings. He had sacrificed his own childhood to ensure their survival—a weight he carried into adulthood. Over those weeks, our bond felt ancient, and my dreams suggested we had known each other in previous lives. This realization didn't just explain his silence; it commanded my respect.

As we continued through various states and towns, I observed the starkly contrasting conditions in which people lived. Yet it was in Mexico City that I encountered a familiar struggle. A group of kids began picking at me simply because I lived in the United States, telling me to go back and that I didn't belong. Remembering my parents' firm advice to avoid trouble, I did my best to ignore them.

Unbeknownst to me, my paternal grandmother had witnessed the bullying from her second-story window. She rushed out and pulled me aside. "You should never let anyone push you around," she instructed. "Never start a fight, but don't ever walk away from one."

A shock of powerful freedom hit me. I turned back to the group of five older boys and challenged them one at a time. I dropped the first three with a precision that felt ancient, my hands moving with a speed I didn't know I possessed. The remaining two took one look at the scene, refused to fight, and quickly disappeared.

When I finally looked at my grandmother, genuine surprise was etched on her face. "Where did you learn to fight like that?" she asked. The truth felt too strange, too risky; I couldn't tell her I remembered it from my dreams.

Soon, every boy for blocks wanted to fight the kid from the United States, and I was more than happy to oblige. Fighting became a daily activity for the rest of my time in Mexico City. I adopted my grandmother's wisdom—never start a fight—but I never walked away from one either. From that point on, I fought with a profound confidence in my ability to defend myself, and I never lost.

The daily conflict on the streets was not my only battle. The intense physicality sharpened my mental state within my dream journey, causing my visions to grow in intensity. The experiences were undeniably real, spanning the extremes of existence: enduring the scorching desert sun and the biting winter cold; savoring the soft summer breeze and the fragrance of spring.

I lived through struggles for survival at sea, the embrace of love and family, and the depths of hate and desperation. Even the physical pain of battle and the acceptance of life or death were vivid. Crucially, my dreams always concluded with a guardian's final decree—a reminder that in this journey, I must not take a life. This warning continued to be reinforced well into my thirties.

Immersed in time with my family during the trip, an intuitive understanding surfaced: I was connected to them in past lives. This sense was consistently affirmed in my dreams. Naively assuming everyone shared these experiences, I felt compelled to share them with my father.

However, a powerful dream intervened. The silhouettes of my guides encircled me, clarifying that every soul has a distinct purpose, a unique role, and its own set of pre-arranged milestones essential for growth.

"The wisdom of knowing other souls' past lives is a sacred insight meant only for you."

With this guidance, confidence settled fully into me. For the first time, I felt truly empowered. I now looked forward to my journey with patience and excitement.

Armed with this clarity, my return to the United States sparked an immediate obsession with contact sports. While I had played organized soccer my whole life, attending a professional football game changed everything. I saw it as the closest thing to genuine hand-to-hand combat without the ultimate consequence, and I was eager to get on the field.

Settling for anything less than a starting position or being the best player was unacceptable. I poured my resolve into the game, fueled by a drive my teammates didn't fully understand. This success in sports became my key; it opened the doors to friends' homes as their parents took a sudden interest in me. I soon understood that their attention was a thinly veiled request for me to protect their children from my physicality on the field.

The start of Junior High was a lightning bolt of excitement and nerves. My main focus wasn't academics, but rather getting involved in school sports. Located at the edge of town, the school drew students from several neighboring communities, creating a broader, more unpredictable world than the one I had known.

While my parents ensured we grew up on a diverse diet of music—from traditional Latin to big band and classical—my own soundtrack during this time was soul and rock 'n' roll. But it was that heavy metal, aggressive sound that truly fueled my eagerness. It was more than just music; it was a rhythmic preparation for the physical challenges ahead. I felt the pounding drums and distorted guitars matching the intensity in my chest—a sonic armor I put on before stepping onto the field.

Standing there, waiting for the whistle, I realized the music, the dreams, and the physical contact were all parts of the same whole. I was finally ready for the new adventure.

The new school environment immediately opened my eyes to the stark reality of social differences. I had been harboring deep feelings about these issues, and I was finally ready to confront them. I welcomed the fact that there were large numbers of students from diverse ethnic groups. While discrimination was still present, it was no longer solely focused on me.

Students quickly separated into groups—a defense mechanism that allowed them to find security and avoid individual harassment. Several of these groups, aside from the White students, asked me to join, promising me their support as a seventh grader. I declined; I wasn't interested in joining any faction.

Declining to align myself with a clique immediately put a target on my back, and I anticipated the conflict. More urgent was the "tradition" of eighth and ninth graders harassing seventh graders. As a new student, I successfully defended myself against the upper-class bullies and their leaders. The constant fighting finally ended after a confrontation with the ninth-grade ringleader, whom I left with a bloody lip and nose. From that day on, I was left alone for the rest of Junior High.

But the experience took a toll. I found myself becoming increasingly disturbed and angry by all forms of bullying and began to feel a compelling need to intervene whenever I saw it happen.

My guides provided clarification on the force behind these emotions. They confirmed that every soul's journey involves confronting trials, and the path of one soul influences all others—affirming that no encounter is ever coincidental.

The intensity of my sympathy and empathy stemmed from feeling the pain of other souls directly. Moving forward, my task was to understand this spiritual reality and gain the self-control necessary to navigate my path successfully.

This intense empathy manifested most strongly when I witnessed boys bullying girls—an offense I could never tolerate. This stance grew from a profound respect for women, rooted in the belief that all souls are equal. I attribute this conviction to having fought side by side with women in past lives, understanding that throughout our various journeys, we have all inhabited both male and female roles.

Because of this ingrained respect, I was never preoccupied with trying to impress girls. Even when I developed a crush, I trusted that any connection deeper than friendship would develop naturally, without the need for performative effort on my part.

My transition into eighth grade brought new friendships, largely through my success in sports and my nature of keeping to myself—I never sought the role of a ringleader.

Yet this period was also defined by the rapid intensification of my premonition dreams. I was now seeing specific futures: the precise cars and motorcycles on the street, complex chains of events, and the exact details of impending mishaps. Compelled to share, I began telling friends and family about these visions before they unfolded. Their response was one of confusion and visible distress; when the predictions came true, they were noticeably shaken.

This discomfort soon turned to anger as they vehemently told me to stop. I was particularly wounded by the intensity of my family's reaction. It was a painful confirmation of my guides' earlier warning: this was a sacred insight meant only for me. From that point on, I understood that my path required a level of internal solitude that even those closest to me could not share.

Finally, I accepted that what I perceive and know is best kept to myself. The deep, familiar feeling of that first day of school echoed in my mind: my journey required self-reliance. I embraced the challenge and the inherent uncertainty of my path, finding solace in my own abilities.

I realized that setting expectations is a solitary act; they belong only to me. As my guides consistently demonstrated, placing expectations on others inevitably leads to disappointment. I began spending my after-school hours listening to music and meditating on my future, secure in the knowledge that it was simply a matter of time before I would be free to fully pursue my purpose.

The counsel from my guides was clear: embrace every experience, regardless of whether it proves easy or difficult. This truth resonated deeply, as I recognized this phase of life from many previous journeys. Revisiting those past challenges in dreams transformed them, allowing me to carry not just lessons, but fond memories into this present cycle. I no longer saw the trauma of previous lives as a burden, but as a rich tapestry of experience that prepared me for what was to come.

Despite this newfound internal clarity, my external life remained in flux. My immediate family moved twice during this period, even as our extended family began arriving in the United States—uncles, aunts, and cousins filling our world.

My father, the oldest in his family and having helped raise his siblings, maintained that self-imposed obligation throughout his life. He was a caring, compassionate man, universally respected for his humor and wisdom, though his generosity sometimes came at a cost to us. My mother, the quiet pillar of support for him and for us, remained the rock we could turn to for open, honest conversation.

Initially, observing the dynamics among our relatives was concerning. My feelings of distance were reinforced by memories of them in Mexico; I found myself growing resentful of what I perceived as their insincerity and arrogance.

However, this intense friction soon led to a breakthrough: I recognized our relationship in a past life. That clarity explained my lack of trust and acted as a key. From this point forward, recognizing past life connections with the souls in my current journey began to occur with greater frequency and piercing clarity.

The guidance from my guides was now falling into place. Their central teaching was simple:

"You must not be judgmental, because you possess the power to prevent the negative energy of others from swaying your path."

My guides instructed me to maintain a necessary distance from anything or anyone that serves as a negation on my journey. It was a vital piece of wisdom that allowed me to move through the world without being of the world—a rule that continues to shape my decisions and my work to this day.

With my path now clearly defined, my focus narrowed to a single obsession: preparing for high school sports. Our freshman class would be the first group of ninth graders to attend the new high school, and I was eager for the change.

For years, my father had refused to let me play organized tackle football, convinced I would get hurt. That refusal was now irrelevant. I was finally going to play for the high school team, and I spent the entire summer running, weightlifting, and bodybuilding with fierce dedication. I knew I would be returning to a primarily White student body, but I was prepared for anything. I was looking forward to the challenges, knowing exactly what to expect.

The summer's intense training went beyond preparing me for football; it spurred a deeper need to define my future beyond high school. I established a clear, long-term goal: to eventually raise a family with a significantly better life than my own. This meant providing my children with greater understanding, more potential, and the accumulated knowledge I planned to gain. This vision was not a wish, but a certainty—a driving force already clear in my dreams—and I began to plan the exact steps to make it a reality.

The start of my freshman year was surprisingly smooth. My reputation—that of a capable athlete who stood his ground—had preceded me. While the upperclassmen maintained their tradition of hazing and discrimination, the hostility never touched me.

This quiet respect allowed me to fully immerse myself in football. Even my teammates, some of whom I knew from junior high, kept a cautious distance. For the first several weeks of practice, they were intensely observant, watching me closely rather than interacting, as if sizing up a new variable in their locker room.

Having longed to play for years, I thrived on the physical contact and rapidly secured a nomination as one of the team captains. My true motivation was ignited during scrimmages against the sophomore and junior varsity teams. Facing them, I knew the only way to earn respect was to outperform them every single down. This realization fueled my drive to be the fastest, strongest, and most devastating hitter in the school.

My performance was undeniable; before long, varsity coaches integrated me into their team practices and had me dressing out for their games. I had bypassed the traditional hierarchy, proving that when you align your physical effort with your internal certainty, the doors of the institution have no choice but to open.

Through my play on special teams in varsity games, I drew the notice of the senior star, the school's best athlete. He saw something in me that others missed and began to vouch for me, eventually inviting me to join the senior players for after-school activities.

Even with his backing, the path wasn't entirely smooth. I often heard the whispers and protests—other players labeling me a "Mexican tag-along." But the senior star refused to listen. His word was absolute: I was to be left alone. Once the other senior players fell in line, a new sense of purpose took hold of me. I allowed myself to believe I could make a tangible difference against the discrimination that plagued the school. I wasn't just playing for myself anymore; I was becoming a symbol that the status quo could no longer ignore.

My growing acceptance of my dreams and inner guidance provided the confidence that I was finally on the right path. I was no longer second-guessing the whispers of my soul; I was walking in alignment with them.

That night, at a school basketball game, friends drew my attention to a group of girls sitting behind us. To them, it was a typical social encounter, but for me, the air was about to change. When we introduced ourselves, my focus narrowed instantly to one girl. The distinct shape of her face, her eyes, and the curve of her forehead triggered a chilling, ancient memory: she was my partner from my life in Greece.

Talking to her after the game and sensing her energy solidified my conviction. It wasn't just a resemblance; it was a resonance. It was her. I didn't feel the need to impress or perform; I was simply overwhelmed by a profound sense of gratitude that our paths had reconnected across the centuries. We were no longer strangers, but travelers meeting again at a prearranged station.

My sophomore summer felt like a sharp reversal. With the previous seniors gone, the new senior class immediately targeted me with aggressive and derogatory attacks. They saw a younger player who had risen too fast, and they intended to put me in my place.

As a starting varsity defensive lineman, I decided my response would be to punish them on the field during every practice. My coaches didn't object; in fact, they ensured I would go head-to-head with my antagonists. They wanted to see if I would break or if I would dominate.

Despite the hostility, the coaches encouraged me to lead the rest of the players. My instinct was clear: I would do what I had always done in my "dream battles" and lead by example alone. I had no interest in directing or motivating; I would let my actions speak for themselves.

Early in high school, my intuitive senses sharpened dramatically. I felt the emotional state of everyone around me—from their joy and health to their deep-seated pain and ill will. This total immersion made me fiercely compassionate, driving me to help others in any way I could.

However, this same sensitivity fueled a powerful impatience toward those who acted with arrogance or selfishness. My nocturnal dreams offered a stark explanation: they vividly depicted past lives where I had been the very individual I now despised—a person with no regard for others or even life itself. I began to sense that my journey carried the weight of a karmic duty, a form of penance for past indiscretions. My current drive to defend the weak was a debt I was paying to the universe.

Yet, my dreams also offered a contrast, showing me past lives dedicated entirely to service: I had been a monk, a priest, and a doctor. These were not random lives; they were the foundation of my current healing and protective nature.

My spiritual guardians were clear:

"The knowledge gained in those service-oriented journeys is essential training for the trials you will face in the near future."

The monk's discipline, the doctor's care, and the warrior's strength were all converging. I would soon understand exactly how necessary that preparation was.

Life, however, often interrupts destiny with the unexpected drama of high school routines. My closest friend met me after class, grinning as he told me he'd already set up a date for me this Friday. I laughed, dismissing the idea instantly. "I'm not interested in blind dates, man. I want nothing to do with it."

"It's not a blind date," he replied. "She's the girl you were talking to at the basketball game last year." Just as the words left his mouth, she suddenly rounded the corner, walking toward us with a huge, wide-eyed smile. Seeing her face—it was her—I completely lost the heart to say no.

My date's Italian-American heritage gave me a moment of calm anticipation before meeting her parents. But as I passed the kitchen window, I was instantly hit by her father's booming, hateful declaration: "No Mexicans are coming into this house!"

I stood frozen on the walkway until the front door flew open. "Let's go," she commanded, rushing out to meet me. The irony of a man from an immigrant background rejecting another minority group was darkly comical. While we enjoyed the movie and shared a connection through our backgrounds, the moment at the door confirmed I had no interest in a second date or entering a world where I was viewed as a negation.

With my dating life uneventful through the remainder of my sophomore year, I turned my focus back to the deeper guidance of my path. At both my school and the crosstown rival, most girls were only interested in dating popular football players, and teachers only encouraged this celebrity culture by being lax with school rules for the athletes.

Despite feeling urged by my guides to embrace every high school experience, I began to feel guilty about taking advantage of the looser academic environment and the lack of engagement from my peers. This emotional conflict ultimately drove me to directly request guidance.

Lying in bed each night, I would ask my questions, and the answers were startlingly immediate. They surfaced in my dreams or arrived unexpectedly—triggered by a person, an event, or a sudden burst of feeling. Although the insights were sometimes scattered, requiring me to connect the separate pieces, the full answer always became clear. This reinforced one crucial truth:

"Time, genuine interaction, and sharp awareness are the keys."

I hadn't missed any vital steps; the entire experience simply required patience and integrity.

By my eighth and ninth-grade years, my summers were already spoken for, working at my uncle's business at my father's insistence. Now, he was escalating his demands: I needed to find a job and start contributing financially to the household.

While our culture dictated that children hand over all their wages for family expenses, I felt differently. I argued that my earnings should cover my personal needs alone—a stance that directly challenged the traditional hierarchy. My mother became my ally in this conflict, successfully negotiating a truce that allowed me to maintain my independence.

I took on this new employment with the same discipline and competitive spirit I reserved for sports. I didn't see it as just a job; I recognized it as the first real step toward the self-sufficiency my path required.

Back at school during the third quarter of my junior year, I started an elective class where I found myself surrounded by girls—a dynamic I, as a popular athlete, was happy to embrace. But then I saw her: the smiley girl I'd taken to the movies a year earlier.

She was a member of the school drill team and, complicating matters, was currently dating a teammate of mine from the football team. In the rigid social hierarchy of high school, this should have been an impassable boundary. Despite the complications, the foundation we had built during our first night at the movies remained. That shared connection evolved into a solid friendship over the course of the year. By the final weeks of the semester, the friendship shifted into something deeper, and we officially started dating.

I was intensely focused on the summer training plans I'd created for my final senior year of football. Unfortunately, my father's commitment had already set a competing path in stone. Because a company had already scheduled me on the assembly line, the arrangement was unalterable. This forced me to miss all summer practices, but the real-world experience I gained proved invaluable.

The daily grind of eight-hour shifts on the assembly line, often alongside people who had performed this physically punishing work for two decades, was a brutal wake-up call. Listening to their stories—their family pressures, ambitions, and limitations—made one thing perfectly clear: this was not the future I wanted for myself. Despite that sharp realization, I walked away with a tremendous and lasting respect for my co-workers. They were warriors of a different kind.

Missing the summer sessions earned me the immediate disapproval of the coaches. I had naïvely expected them to be understanding, and their negative reaction was a swift, sharp reminder of my guardian's most important lesson:

"You cannot expect others to meet your expectations."

The real instruction from my guides was to stop being upset with the coaches and start being upset with myself for setting the expectation at all—a realization I have consciously had to re-learn throughout my life.

This experience immediately changed my dreams. They began to twist, focusing on past-life responsibilities and my relationships with others—both how I had handled them and how I needed to move forward. This new focus rapidly dissolved my obsession with sports; the ambition to be a professional athlete no longer seemed vital.

The main message, however, was clear and actionable:

"Apply the 100% dedication I once gave to sports to every other goal you want to accomplish."

The leniency given to the popular school athlete finally ran out. My senior year was a rude awakening, forcing a frantic scramble to complete the required studies I had casually dismissed in previous years. I was no longer the "celebrity" being carried by the system; I was a student facing the reality of my own neglect.

But with the end of the football season came a new, serious focus. I immediately secured a job to begin saving for my post-high school education and purchased a motorcycle to establish my self-sufficiency. This commitment extended to my personal life; I was now diligently investing in my relationship with my girlfriend, determined to build the future I had seen in my dreams.

Graduation day was finally here, bringing a potent mix of thrill and apprehension for the unknown road ahead. The feeling instantly conjured memories of the long-ago elementary and junior high days I spent impatiently waiting for this single moment of release.

Alongside the rush of freedom, an unexpected and intense appreciation settled over me. I looked back at the teachers and coaches who had marked my journey—the ones who supported me and the ones who challenged me—and realized they were all essential to my molding.

My trusted guides consistently reminded me that this deep gratitude would be a cornerstone for my future success. I was to carry no resentment forward, only the strength of the lessons I had learned.

At home, the house had grown quieter. Only my oldest sister, my niece, and I remained, as my youngest sister had long since married and moved out. After graduation, the discipline I had shown at my summer job paid off: my employer offered me a significant full-time position and a promotion.

Having witnessed the countless sacrifices my parents made to bring us here and keep us together, I reached a quiet, firm decision. I didn't want to be another burden on their space; I wanted to move out so they could finally enjoy the privacy they had earned over decades of labor. While it was challenging for them to accept my departure—as children in Latino culture often stay until they marry—I knew it was the right step for our family. I wasn't leaving out of a desire to escape, but out of a profound respect for the life they had built. It was my final act of childhood and my first act of true adulthood.

My high school sweetheart and I shared mutual goals, making her parents' prejudiced views toward other groups irrelevant to my feelings. This was an issue she had to manage within her own family, and I continually assured her of my support. I understood this difficult dynamic would likely persist, so I chose to be her peace rather than another source of conflict.

With my new independent life established, I moved into the city's largest and newest apartment complex, landing a spot in the development's most sought-after location.

I was no longer a boy waiting for his life to begin; I was a man with the resources and the resolve to dictate his own destiny with a deliberate step toward the life I had promised myself.

CHAPTER IV

The London Echoes

Past-life regressions and the recognition of ancient combat connections

Four months into my independent life, fully engaged with family and friends, I prepared to implement the ambitious plans I'd drafted. Yet despite my readiness, powerful dreams and internal feelings began pushing me to reassess my goals. Unsettled by this sudden uncertainty, I immediately asked my guardians for a clear sign.

Later one night, while watching the news alone, a story unfolded about a young man struggling after losing his leg in a motorcycle accident. A question hit me instantly, as if whispered: What would you do if this were you? The sign was undeniable. My internal answer was immediate: I would handle it, drawing on the strength gained from surviving far worse trials in previous lives.

On Wednesday, October 18, 1978, I almost made a fatal mistake. Rushing to work and determined not to be late, I consciously left my motorcycle helmet behind. I didn't always wear it, and at the time the omission seemed insignificant. Yet as the elevator doors began to close, a sudden, powerful chill and a feeling of dread washed over me.

This was no mere anxiety; it was an undeniable premonition. I had to have the helmet. I stepped back and retrieved it, making a split-second decision that would ultimately save my life.

Nearing the end of my shift, the owner unexpectedly asked me to deliver some special-ordered equipment. I agreed to the three-hour round trip, canceling my gym plans without a second thought. When I finally returned and secured the company vehicle, the sky had darkened into twilight. As I zipped my helmet into place, I felt a sudden, profound shift—an odd certainty of impending change. It felt as if I were standing at the very edge of a new beginning, though I could not yet see the cliff.

Four blocks from work, I made the familiar turn onto the two-lane residential street. I noticed a line of halted cars ahead, headlights glaring, stuck behind a single vehicle that refused to move halfway down the block. The street was narrow, leaving no room to navigate the bottleneck. I hugged the right side of my lane, inched toward the parked cars, and began flashing my high beams to signal my approach.

An elderly woman in an older model car at the front of the line was causing the snarl. The moment I drew parallel, she swung her car quickly and unexpectedly left, directly into me. Her bumper crushed my leg instantly, vaulting me over the hood. Time seemed to stop; everything moved in disorienting slow motion. Behind me, the sound of my motorcycle scraping the pavement turned the street into a flurry of sparks and light, followed by the sickening impact as I hit the asphalt and began to roll uncontrollably.

Unsure if cars were bearing down on me, I stuck my arms out to halt my slide. As I scraped forward on my hands and knees, I recognized the severity of the damage: I could feel my leg rotating unnaturally against the rough asphalt, and my knees were already on fire from the friction. I saw the stream of passing headlights as I scraped by until the force of the slide ripped through the fingertips of my gloves. The sudden, shocking contact of bare skin on the road forced me back into a helpless roll before I finally came to a grinding, painful stop.

I forced myself up immediately, clutching my fractured left leg to hop out of the path of traffic. Looking over my shoulder, I saw my motorcycle lying mid-road, its headlight still casting a beam onto a surreal sight: a cloud of white feathers drifting down from a deep tear in my down jacket. The absurdity of the situation—the comical plume against the backdrop of the wreck—was a moment of painful irony as I struggled to clear the lane.

I reached the sidewalk and slumped, clutching my leg. The sight was brutal: my shredded pant leg dripped blood, and my foot was twisted backward. The pain hit—a blinding, white-hot shock. Just as a scream clawed its way up my throat, a figure cut through the glare of the headlights: a little boy, perhaps seven years old, walking toward me with a serious, curious expression.

I was not going to break down in front of him. I swallowed the scream and held the agony at bay.

People immediately swarmed me, spilling from cars and surrounding homes. I searched the crowd for the little boy, but he was gone. Amid the chaos of paramedics and police, the elderly driver who had hit me approached. Tears streamed down her face, her expression a mix of anguish and terror. The officer holding my hand leaned in. "This is the driver who hit you," he said quietly. "She's eighty-nine years old."

A wave of pity washed over me, instantly dissolving any potential for anger. Seeing her distress, a complete calmness settled over me. My focus shifted away from the wreckage and toward the path ahead; my only thought now was the hospital.

At the hospital, I was told the on-call surgeon was finishing a procedure and would see me soon to approve the necessary pain medication. Still lying on the gurney in the X-ray room, I turned my head and saw the images on the screen. My lower leg looked like shattered eggshells.

A nurse noticed my gaze, leaned down, and said quietly, "Your leg will need to be amputated."

The news was strangely irrelevant. Having lived past lives and lost limbs before, the threat didn't register as a true loss. My soul felt intact, even if my body was broken. My only concern was the immediate next step: securing medication and beginning the work that needed to be done.

I was moved to a waiting area, my full-face helmet placed on a nearby chair. It was utterly destroyed. A deep, continuous scratch ran across the entire left side, from the visor to the back—an undeniable record of the impact. That ruined shell confirmed the powerful chill and sudden dread I'd felt that morning. It was the physical evidence of my guardians' protection.

Suddenly, I realized the crash sequence had mirrored the slow-motion action I had only ever experienced in my past-life battle dreams. Revisiting that fluid, slowed sequence in my mind didn't bring fear; it brought an odd, comforting sense of familiarity. I had been here before.

After a grueling hour and twenty minutes of waiting—with various doctors checking my leg—I noticed a medic examining me with unusual intensity. I immediately sensed an "old soul" about him. When I asked how much longer until the surgeon arrived, the nurse replied, "He is the surgeon."

Only then was I finally given a pain shot. He gravely informed me we were going into surgery and that he would do everything possible to save my leg, though the chances were fifty-fifty. He asserted it would be a long, difficult battle. Despite the initial relief doing little for the pain, I simply wanted to get started.

Later that night, the attending surgeon came to my bedside. He cut a striking figure in a salt-and-pepper suit, carrying a black medical bag, and possessed a supremely calm and confident air—the welcome presence of an old soul. He laid out the timeline: my stay would be long, I would be moved to a private room, and further surgeries were necessary.

The surgeon promised I would be his first priority in the morning and his last at night—a promise he never broke. When he asked about my pain, I told him it was gone. A genuine curiosity creased his brow; he confessed he had never seen a patient with this specific injury fail to react to that level of agony. I kept my reply brief, claiming a high pain tolerance, and dared not mention that I had survived far worse in other lifetimes.

The cycle of surgery was taxing—two procedures every week. In the recovery room after my sixth operation, the seclusion became overwhelming. I began to contemplate the life I'd left outside and the absence of my old routine. Though I knew this was my path, the weight of the moment finally crystallized into a direct question: "Why this?"

It was my first true query—my first active search for meaning. With that question, a deep, quiet calm descended. I accepted that this was only the prologue; I had to be patient and watch for the signs of what came next. I recognized that my strength now needed to be directed outward, helping my family manage their own grief over my condition. My path was no longer about my leg; it was about my legacy.

For weeks, my nights were dominated by terrifying dreams. They featured a relentless reel of fatal near-misses from my time on a motorcycle—accidents that could have claimed my life, initiated by other drivers or my own mistakes.

The dream sequence always spiraled, violently jolting me awake in a cold sweat as I relived the final moments of the crash. Each time, however, the fear was instantly replaced by a powerful, insistent realization: the elderly lady and this catastrophic accident had actually preserved my life, establishing a crucial chain of events needed for me to fulfill my intended path. But a deeper question remained: Why was I being preserved? What was I being saved for?

My hospital stay evolved into a journey of deep soul searching, catalyzed by daily visits from the hospital nuns. Arranged at my mother's request, they gently urged me to pray. Although I politely declined formal prayer, I welcomed the opportunity for long, meaningful conversations.

Despite my complicated history with Catholic school, I remained respectful, acknowledging their genuine, well-meaning intent. I had always believed in God, but it was through these daily dialogues that my specific beliefs emerged with clarity. The power of this revelation ultimately prompted me to seek direct verification from my spiritual guardians.

The answers from my guardians arrived through both dreams and thoughts, providing deep reassurance. They confirmed the existence of a Supreme Being to whom every living soul is accountable. This entity guides us throughout our lives and after we cross over to return "home." Everything in the universe is His creation, intrinsically connected as one.

This core confirmation would be reinforced throughout the rest of my life. With my internal world fundamentally reordered, my attention could finally turn outward.

The extended duration of my hospitalization fostered a meaningful friendship with the nursing staff. My private room became a quiet haven where they frequently joined me for their lunch breaks. During these shared moments—whether we were talking, listening to music, or simply watching TV—I listened as they opened up about their lives. This close proximity heightened my awareness, allowing me to perceive their emotional spectrum: their energy, pain, joy, fear, and confidence. It revealed the unique soul stage of each person's journey.

Witnessing their resilience made me acutely aware that I needed to find the truth of my own soul's path.

I spent hours immersed in music, each melody serving as a powerful trigger that transported me back through the past nineteen years. These deep, musical recollections, along with dreams that vividly reinforced past events, confirmed a powerful, inherent ability I had long underestimated. The insight was suddenly sharp and undeniable.

The message was simple but profound:

Define your strengths and your weaknesses. Accept your flaws as part of yourself, dedicate yourself to improving them, and harness your gifts to create positive momentum in your life.

In this quest for direction, I realized I had already established a profound connection with the man orchestrating my physical return to the world.

My strongest bond in the hospital was with my surgeon. Though his 6 a.m. visits were brief, his dedication was absolute; he often stayed for an hour or more during his midnight rounds. This afforded us time for long conversations, where I peppered him with medical questions while he inquired about my life. Beyond his professional mastery, he was a genuinely compassionate man who quietly supported local schools.

Every visit, morning or night, he wore the distinct "salt-and-pepper" suit that had become his signature among the entire hospital staff.

Finally, the time for dialogue ended and the professional mandate began. After three months and thirty-two surgeries, my surgeon announced I was going home—but not without conditions. The release came with a critical requirement: a full leg cast to be worn until the bone grafts set. As he outlined the strict recovery schedule, he warned me of the significant challenge of adjusting to the abrupt end of months of pain medication.

More sobering still, he confirmed the need for future surgeries and maintained my odds at fifty-fifty for keeping my leg. He offered no predictions regarding permanent limitations. For reasons I couldn't explain, this entire prognosis felt deeply familiar—as if I had heard it in another life, in another war.

Returning home meant facing new emotional complications. Seeing the toll my ordeal had taken on my parents, I felt a strong need to move out as soon as possible. Their own increasing medical issues reinforced this decision; I refused to become a burden. Despite the immense emotional support from my parents and my high-school sweetheart, my drive for independence demanded immediate action. I needed to push forward on my unique path, and I wanted her by my side as I did.

Two months later, I moved back into the same apartment complex, securing a better unit. The relief of being back where I started was immense, but it immediately gave way to the difficult waiting game of healing. To keep busy, I focused on furnishing the space and establishing a routine. It was during this time that my sweetheart and I decided she would move in with me. Yet despite these positive steps, the uncertainty of my physical limitations made it a struggle to focus on any long-term plans.

A full year passed, marked by the constant burden of a leg cast and zero healing progress. Frustrated by the medical stalemate, I sought answers through intensive meditation. The resulting epiphany was instantaneous and forceful.

The guidance was clear:

Stop looking for sympathy or validation. Acknowledge that no one could comprehend the depth of your unique physical and emotional struggle. The true shift lies in accepting this solitude. Reject external influence, accept your reality, and place your faith entirely in your own purpose.

Only through this deep, internal commitment could I break free. The truth was stark: I could not rely on anyone's predictions—not even my surgeon's. My limitations would be entirely self-imposed.

Therefore, I committed to full responsibility: any failure resulting from this challenge would be mine to claim, and any success would be mine to create. My only remaining task was to patiently wait for the healing or the loss to finalize and then—without hesitation—continue my path forward.

As the second year of the waiting game drew to a close, I finally received the news I had fought for: my bone graft had healed. My cast was replaced with a brace, giving me mobility for the first time in two years.

I immediately channeled my frustration into action, making the gym my primary focus. I pursued my rehabilitation with aggressive intensity, treating every doctor's appointment like an interrogation and every physical-therapy session like a competitive sport. Within just six months, I shed the brace entirely and began to run—a sight that brought visible excitement to my surgeon.

With my physical limitations finally defined, I could focus on the future. I closed the door on sports, accepting they were no longer an option. Marriage and starting a family were soon to follow, but I was faced with a more urgent reality: the health and financial security of my parents. To honor everything they had done for me, I invested in a business alongside them. While I didn't plan on a major operational role, I began actively exploring new career opportunities and continuing my education.

My search for professional purpose began with a commitment to understanding the workings of the mind. I initially explored human psychology, but my research took an unexpected turn when I encountered a book on animal behavior—specifically, dog psychology. I was instantly captivated.

The principles felt deeply familiar. I could immediately discern the flaws and truths within established philosophies, as if I were simply remembering a language I already spoke. This connection drove me to spend countless hours reading every available text on breeds, training, competition, and psychology.

I immersed myself in the library, researching engineering, business, law, history, medicine, and politics. This broad familiarity instilled a great sense of confidence; it showed me that my professional options were vast. Yet, despite these possibilities, the undeniable pull of working with dogs remained constant. I needed to reconnect with them.

When I asked my spiritual guardians for insight into this obsession, the answer arrived in a vivid dream: a detailed memory of a past life in WWII London.

I was a young English sentry with a German Shepherd companion. We were inseparable, until we were both lost during a bombing raid.

My path was finally clear. I would launch a dog-training business specializing in personal protection and police work. I was not just starting a career; I was continuing a partnership that the bombs of London could not break. To master the trade with absolute precision, I secured a grueling schedule: full-time security guard, part-time veterinary assistant, and obedience trainer at a boarding kennel.

This commitment required a painful sacrifice. Telling my parents I would no longer be involved in their business was difficult and hard for them to accept. I explained my undeniable drive to follow the work I felt a deep, spiritual passion for. Acceptance finally came when they realized my ambition was the same restless, vital force that had compelled my father to leave everything behind to come to the United States. I wasn’t rejecting them; I was honoring the very spirit they had given me.

My fiancée and I had temporarily moved in with my older brother to help care for my niece and nephew while he completed graduate school. We were on the threshold of our own future, standing on the edge of the life I had planned during those long months in the hospital. The "waiting game" was over. The work was about to begin.

CHAPTER V

The Latticework

Resonance, responsibility, and navigating the "Superfund" of the human soul

Following our wedding on July 3, 1982, we relocated to a secluded cabin retreat in the mountains. As I prepared to launch my dog training business, my primary goal was isolation: to shield us from negative influences and dedicate my focus entirely to our future and starting a family.

This solitude allowed me to perfect the training of my dogs, but more importantly, it provided a quiet space for deep meditation. In that silence, I began to foresee and dictate the exact actions required for my success. I was not guessing at the future; I was drafting it.

This quiet focus did more than sharpen my business plan; it opened a new channel of awareness. My dreams, which I now experienced with vivid intensity, were focused entirely on my first twenty-three years—illuminating the mechanics of my struggles, successes, fears, and insecurities, as well as my drive and resolve. During this time, the presence of past relatives became a constant, comforting reality.

They appeared to comfort, encourage, or simply reinforce their presence. Sometimes they spoke; other times, I simply felt the weight of their message. I soon realized that when I saw them, I only needed to speak directly to them—they were active participants in my journey.

Through this channel, my guardians revealed a staggering truth:

Every soul willingly agrees to the challenges of its journey on Earth, including the impact it will have on others and the time allotted for that life. Crucially, we choose the souls we encounter—we select our parents and siblings before the journey begins. Furthermore, both before and after we cross over, we continue to look after living souls, guiding them and, in a sense, living through them in the physical world.

The reason we lack memory of these agreements is the very basis of our growth. The choices we make at every crossroads—whether for better or worse—are the raw materials of our eventual life review.

Anchored by these truths and a newly defined purpose, I immersed myself in my work with a passion I knew I would never find in any other profession. My connection to the dogs was immediate and profound. It was not long before a reputation for excellence preceded me, and my training business began to thrive.

I secured contracts with several police departments, collaborating with a trainer who supplied their K-9 units. My schedule grew demanding: I conducted seminars for dog clubs and worked alongside the top trainers and judges for police dog competitions, all while managing my own private clientele.

My constant, internal communication with the dogs became the crucial lens through which I interpreted the hidden struggles and emotional imbalances of their human companions. The dynamics I witnessed were both intriguing and telling. While the effort to build a life together was often evident, truly comprehending the dog-human bond remained a challenge for most. I could feel their frustration, their confusion, and—in many cases—a fundamental lack of genuine effort.

This led to a pivotal realization: I was training the client far more than the dog. I became so acutely attuned that I could discern a person's character simply by observing their animal, often before a single word was exchanged. The dog was the lens through which the human soul was made visible.

My guardians swiftly confirmed this burgeoning awareness—this ability to feel a client's innermost emotions. They explained that the entire universe is bound by a latticework of energy and vibration, connecting every living thing. While some individuals possess a natural resonance with the ocean, the forest, or the soil, they clarified my specific place within this web: my deep, singular connection was with the canine world.

This confirmation became my anchor. It replaced my lingering doubts with a fierce confidence, freeing me to fully embrace my purpose: providing comfort and guidance to those in need through the lens of the dog.

Thirteen days after my twenty-fifth birthday—on December 8, 1983—we welcomed our first daughter. I felt the connection instantly. She was an old soul, a kindred spirit with whom I had already traversed many lifetimes in various roles. This shared history was a truth I felt immediately—one that would be continually confirmed throughout my life.

Anchored by this soul connection, the responsibility of a growing family intensified my dedication to securing a better future. This goal justified my decision to intentionally distance my family from negative influences—even when it meant separating from extended relatives to preserve the sanctuary I was building. This new stage of life compelled me to prioritize my children's interests above my own; a commitment made in my youth that I was now profoundly grateful to fulfill.

To secure the best resources, my wife and I moved to a growing community with newly constructed schools. However, after two years of rapid success, my work schedule became unsustainable. I was starting at 6 a.m. and often arriving home after midnight. Recognizing the need for balance, I decided to take a temporary break. I accepted a low-stress, part-time role to rest and plan a relaunch, confident in my ability to rebuild my self-employment when the time was right.

Seeking a better work-life balance, I accepted a role at a hazardous waste site with the exact schedule I needed: eight hours a day, five days a week.

The interview was conducted by the operations manager, and I immediately recognized his energy. He was an "old soul"—a man with a strong, positive presence who looked through me with immediate trust. Aware that I had no background in environmental work, he dedicated surprisingly little time to technical questions. Instead, his focus shifted to my character and my experience running a successful business.

I felt as though he was looking straight through the job title of Environmental Technician and into my core. The spiritual connection we shared created immediate mutual trust; his tone remained one of comfort and assurance throughout. As he handed me four massive binders detailing the environmental control systems and protocols, I realized that this sixty-five-year-old man not only commanded respect but gave it freely. He was the sole decision maker, and he had chosen me.

I was given three days to review the materials before starting that Monday. As I opened the first of the three-inch binders, I was astonished by my immediate comprehension. I didn't just understand the content; I speed-read the remaining three binders, grasping complex engineering aspects with total clarity. It was a retrieval of expertise I had mastered in a previous journey. I was ready to walk onto that site not as a novice, but as an expert returning to the field.

Despite this newfound knowledge, the reality of my first day was a shock. The atmosphere felt less like a professional environment and more like junior high school. My department was utterly disorganized, with coworkers openly competing for dominance. Our manager, a recent college graduate my own age, lacked both the experience and the respect of the crew.

Because the site was so fragmented, collaboration was nonexistent. My strategy was straightforward: focus solely on my work, avoid the prevalent drug dealings, and ensure I always wore my Personal Protective Equipment

(PPE)—a safety measure virtually ignored by everyone else in that hazardous environment.

It was not long before others across the site began to harass me for my consistent use of PPE, arguing that my adherence to safety made them look bad. While I sought to avoid unnecessary conflict, I refused to jeopardize my safety for the sake of their ego. Because disputes there were often settled after hours, I established firm boundaries quickly. Soon, they left me alone—and more importantly, other workers began wearing their own PPE, following the standard I had set.

I also felt compelled to address the prevalent drug activity. I physically ensured the dealers understood they were to stay away from the workers in my department; I knew their compromised judgment could endanger my life or the lives of my crew.

As the environment stabilized, my fascination with the control systems grew. I began suggesting improvements for testing and optimization that yielded immediate, excellent results, establishing my credibility almost overnight. Simultaneously, the workplace began to clear; personnel changes purged the dealers and troublemakers from my department. This success did not go unnoticed. The Operations Manager personally approached me to offer me the role of Environmental Department Leadman. Remembering my ultimate goal of returning to my own business, I told him I would seriously consider the offer, weighing the security of the role against the calling of my future.

Accepting the offer required a philosophical shift. My thoughts immediately turned to my football days, when I had always stood firm on the principle of leading by example rather than simply directing or motivating others to act. I began to ponder the full responsibility of the Leadman role: if I took this position, could I truly influence these workers' lives in a profound, positive, and productive way? The magnitude of that possibility was deeply intriguing.

The following day, the Operations Manager called me into his office for my decision. Before I could speak, he clarified the terms of the promotion. In addition to a significant pay increase, the position carried one key requirement: I would have to pursue further education in all engineering disciplines relevant to the company, with the company covering the full cost.

This was a condition I hadn't anticipated, but I realized immediately it was an offer I could not refuse. The decision was sealed.

My focus shifted instantly to the direction and safety of my team. I ensured that every new member grasped the gravity of our work and the absolute necessity of personal safety within a hazardous environment. Simultaneously, my spiritual guides reinforced that I was on the correct path. My premonition dreams now shifted: they centered not only on the individuals I encountered, but on the impending emotional challenges and personal deficits that would test the very core of my resolve.

As I completed my engineering and executive management education, my responsibilities expanded across the company's operations. Eager to see me in a more influential role, the Operations Manager insisted I accept the position of Assistant Safety Director—a move I felt would solidify my internal direction.

I was now tasked with reviewing and approving all site work plans and procedures. This gave me the direct authority to influence personnel attitudes toward their own safety and the safety of others. As I had anticipated, this responsibility was met with significant resistance.

My dreams began to precisely pinpoint individuals on a collision course with tragedy. Those facing deep emotional deficits or in need of a radical attitude adjustment were easy to detect. I meticulously observed their movements and relentlessly reinforced safety protocols, but for some, it was to no avail. In their willful disregard for my efforts, they eventually made fatal errors. I was left to deal with the aftermath alone; no one else in the company—including the acting Safety Director—would take responsibility.

These incidents forced me to confront the absolute end result of non-compliance. During my tenure, I responded to nine fatalities. Each time, I was the first—and often the only—person to arrive. In eight of those cases, the scene was horrifyingly clear: their deaths were the direct result of the exact behaviors I had repeatedly warned them against.

In every instance, as I stood over the scene, I would feel their presence—often sensing them standing right next to me. Knowing they had just "crossed over" and were embarking on a new path, I would share my final thoughts with them. The message from my guardians was a consistent reminder:

It was simply their time—the moment they had agreed to before this journey began. I had to accept the finality of it and learn that our specific paths, once chosen, are largely beyond our control.

These experiences fostered a profound appreciation for the value of our soul's purpose and the interconnected influence we have on one another's journeys. This truth was brought vividly home through my own prophetic dreams: my visions of death always concluded with me standing over my own lifeless body, calmly observing the living before turning to walk away.

In these visions, I had a total grasp of the journey's motivation. The contrast was striking: all human feelings—need, anger, pain, pride, and sadness—were gone, supplanted by a sensation of absolute, warm peace.

This serenity was short-lived. On April 19, 1988, five months after my twenty-ninth birthday, our second daughter was born. As I watched her and listened to her first cry in the delivery room, I instantly recognized her soul. I had known her before in this ongoing journey. This recognition was followed immediately by a directive from my guardians: I was to ensure she accomplished the unmet milestones set for her in this life. The sudden, overwhelming surge of responsibility made it clear—this was a mission I absolutely could not fail.

I felt an undeniable, powerful bond—a mutual influence that promised to propel both of our souls toward continued growth. Yet, for the first time, this potential brought a fear of the responsibility and the possibility of failure. My guardians quickly reassured me: every soul who becomes a parent inherently senses their child's limits, struggles, and strengths. The signs of a soul in need are always obvious.

Armed with the magnitude of the mission before me and the need to secure a stable foundation for my family, I finally implemented a long-planned professional move. I had deliberately waited for my daughter's birth to proceed with this career change. At my previous role, I had established a successful track record, improving collaboration between departments and making safety paramount.

Most importantly, the respect I earned from the personnel confirmed that I had influenced their lives in a profound, positive, and productive way—a core focus I intended to maintain for the remainder of my career.

I accepted a new role with the owner of an engineering consulting firm—a professional I had worked alongside for several years. He was launching an environmental department after securing a national Superfund contract, and both the position and the salary increase were satisfactory.

Crucially, the move allowed me to focus primarily on the physical remediation of the environment. However, once the transition was finalized, the owner backed out of our salary agreement. While his broken promise enraged me, the counsel of my guardians resonated more strongly: I was angrier at myself for allowing a personal history of trust to supersede my natural caution.

Stung by this oversight, my focus shifted inward. My dreams became dominated by visions of past lives—vivid memories of similar betrayals and the critical decisions I had made in previous leadership roles. These were choices that had led both to great success and, ultimately, to death.

My guardians returned to reinforce a crucial lesson:

Every decision carries a consequence, including the decision not to act. They stressed that the risks we take on our journey are always justified by the wisdom we gain. The path forward was now undeniably clear.

Informed by this resolve, my first decisive act was to leverage the company's reliance on my team and me. As the new projects launched, I re-hired my former crews; my reputation preceded me, and it was widely known that my staff and I were being heavily recruited by competing firms.

Faced with the reality of his mistake, the owner was forced to negotiate. He presented me with a written contract granting me full control over project scheduling and budgets, guaranteeing annual pay increases for my staff and ensuring their continued education. This was a sound investment from which the company stood to profit greatly. I didn't just recover my salary; I secured my sovereignty.

With my authority solidified, my focus remained on the high-quality execution of our work and the absolute safety of my crews. As we managed these national Superfund projects, we began to interface with the highest levels of environmental consulting, including those advising the federal government.

We took pride in the fact that my crews stood out for their deep knowledge, efficiency, and professionalism. In contrast, the tactics used by competing firms to gain the trust of clients and government agencies were often tense, unprofessional—and, in many cases, outright dirty.

Driven by an unshakable confidence in my technical correctness, I grew intrigued by the personal attacks and maneuvers used by these competitors during our weekly meetings. My dreams became constant warnings from my guardians regarding these looming strikes. In these sessions, I didn't just anticipate their moves; I successfully disputed and countered every effort to undermine me. It wasn't long before the client began to seek my counsel on all site activities, eventually appointing me as their direct liaison with the government agencies.

My dream warnings didn't just expose professional threats; they opened a profound awareness of human energy, true intent, and deep insecurities. I realized that any positive influence I had on colleagues or competitors would be temporary at best—a truth that confirmed the focus and effort I dedicated to my family was paramount.

As I had often felt before, the sense of imminent change returned. But this time, I was ready to accept it fully when the moment arrived.

And arrive it did—not as a whisper of fate, but as a chilling, undeniable presence. I had been alert for any hint of transition, yet the most significant one was already staring me down. While I had always perceived spirits on my journey, I had also meticulously maintained my distance—a choice rooted in a deep, lingering discomfort that I could no longer ignore.

The rules had suddenly shifted. Sightings were occurring with daily frequency, and more unsettling still, they were no longer ignoring me. They made eye contact and approached, clearly intending to communicate. The experience was a shock of cold adrenaline; I flatly refused to engage, silently ordering them to vanish.

My usual strategy was simple: sense them, avoid eye contact, and carry on. That routine shattered late one night in my office. I felt a familiar presence just beyond the door and stared at the empty frame until a figure stepped into view: my maternal grandfather, his expression calm yet stern.

Unlike the daily encounters with spirits that sought to communicate, this was different. Most entities I encountered were a distinct, translucent bluish-gray—easy to look through—but he was as solid as I was. I sensed no impressions, no emotional residue—just presence. Just as quickly as he appeared, he stepped out of sight. He repeated these silent visits for weeks until the realization finally hit me: he wasn't there to frighten me or deliver a complex message. He simply wanted me to know he was with me.

My grandfather and I had been distant during his life; my childhood exuberance seemed a constant interruption to his quiet. When I was ten, knowing he was dying of lung cancer, I made one final visit. That day was the only time he ever pulled me aside to genuinely speak with me.

His subsequent spiritual visits transformed my understanding of the deceased. The paralyzing fear vanished. I was no longer frightened; I became entirely willing to listen to the spirits who approached. While I began to understand the purpose behind their visits, I chose to keep those communications strictly to myself.

Unlike my grandfather, my maternal grandmother and I shared a close, unbreakable bond. Both were "old souls," but my grandmother possessed special gifts: she was a renowned healer and fortune teller. Through her, I understood that my abilities were not an anomaly, but a legacy.

My grandmother would often share her experiences and communications with spirits—conversations I always understood intuitively. When she passed away, my parents decided I shouldn't attend the burial, believing the loss would affect me too deeply. While her passing left a significant void, her stories had served as a quiet preparation for everything that was to come. She had given me the maps for a territory I was only just beginning to settle.

My office was situated on a Superfund site, bordered by a highway and a diverse set of neighbors: a cemetery, a nursery, a junkyard, and an active construction site. My morning ritual required a full inspection of the site and operating equipment.

Driving up the east hill, I was hit by an uncontrollable urge to look left, directly across the highway. Something was aggressively demanding my attention, though I couldn't yet comprehend why. I drove to the summit, seeking a higher vantage point to scan the chaotic landscape beyond the road.

My gaze bypassed the nursery, the junkyard, and the construction site, snapping instantly to the cemetery. There, at the corner beside the fence line, my vision hyper-focused on a figure glowing with an intense, radiant yellow light. It felt as if my consciousness left my body and surged across the highway to meet it.

Standing before me, arms extended and a smile on her face, was my grandmother—but decades younger, as she would have looked in her mid-thirties. The unmistakable strength of our bond rushed through me. Staring at her radiant face, I instinctively whispered, "I love you," and was violently thrust back into my body.

She was instantly gone.

Shocked, thrilled, and suddenly panicked by the reality of the vision, I returned to the office and immediately called my mother. I asked for the name of the cemetery where my grandmother was buried; it was the exact one I had been staring at. I cut short my mother's frantic questions, promised to call her back, and sped directly to the site.

I drove to the exact corner by the fence line where she had appeared. There, precisely where the radiant yellow light had stood, was her grave marker. I looked back across the highway to the spot where I had pulled over earlier, gaining the undeniable, physical confirmation I needed.

Even with that proof, the sheer force of this spiritual awakening was so intense that I began to question my sanity, struggling for a rational explanation. My guides intervened in my dreams, reassuring me of the purpose behind my past life knowledge. Their directive was clear: I was to refocus my energy and attention solely on the grounding realities of this present journey.

This realization forced me to confront a growing disappointment: the pervasive lack of empathy and the malicious actions I saw daily, all driven solely by personal gain. As my respect for these individuals vanished, I became highly selective, focusing my support only on those I felt deserved it—an approach I would carry through the rest of my career, regardless of the inevitable retaliation.

I grew impatient. I understood that playing these cynical games would never allow me to achieve my true goal: cleaning the environment. When the president of the firm created by the responsible companies approached me with a proposal to form a spin-off and manage site operations internally, I believed it was the opening I needed. I accepted the position without hesitation, hoping to finally install effective environmental control systems.

Soon after the transition, I began communicating more directly with government agencies. During a private lunch with several agency heads, I asked them directly: Why was there such hesitation to approve new systems for immediate contamination cleanup?

Their reply was delivered with chilling sincerity: their primary responsibility was the study of environmental effects, not the final cleanup. Remediation would only begin once they had obtained sufficient data. They ended the conversation with a polite acknowledgment of my concerns, leaving me with the stark realization that our priorities were fundamentally unreconcilable.

The agency's revelation made my path forward indisputable. My guides' directive—to refocus my energy solely on the grounding realities of this journey—now resonated with a heavy finality. I could no longer remain.

My focus shifted immediately to preparing my staff for my departure, ensuring they were equipped to continue their journey without me. After months of grueling sixteen-hour days, I took a much-needed two-week vacation, which naturally evolved into a period of total, unfiltered dedication to my family.

On May 27, 1992, six months after my thirty-fourth birthday, we welcomed our son into the world. I felt an immediate, powerful connection; he was an old soul, just like my father, and I was certain our paths had crossed in many lives before this one. His birth—a truly momentous occasion—was juxtaposed against a difficult physical struggle: I was battling a serious infection in my left leg at the time.

The infection was not new, but after fifteen years, its spreading demanded an immediate consultation with my surgeon. The news was extensive: the hardware that had supported me for over a decade now had to be removed. I faced six weeks of heavy antibiotics and, critically, the surgeries to finally rebuild my knee.

During the months of recovery—a period in which I continued to work—the painful realization of how much time I had lost with my daughters struck me with staggering force. It was a defining moment; I made a firm commitment to change my priorities and ensure that such a sacrifice would never happen again.

This commitment was tested almost immediately. Following my recovery, the company's dynamics deteriorated rapidly. The head of the firm chose to enforce control through a management style of intimidation, fracturing collaboration among the staff.

My initial requirement for transitioning to this company had been the maintenance of my current contract with a pay increase. I was prepared to complete that term and leave, but the situation quickly became untenable. I was asked to omit information, to lie on official reports, and to allow contracts to deviate from their established terms. I refused to compromise my integrity, fully anticipating the professional consequences.

Upon returning from a two-week vacation, I noticed immediate and concerning changes: several shelves of archives were missing. Before I could investigate, I was summoned to a meeting with the company head. He requested, one final time, that I alter the cost breakdown for a closeout report.

I politely refused. In response, I was informed that my position had been eliminated. Since I still had several months remaining on my contract, the termination effectively became a welcome, extended paid vacation. I walked away from the Superfund site for the last time, taking my integrity, my pride, and my future with me.

While my departure was an obvious concern to my wife, my guides offered immediate reassurance: I was on the right path, and all would work out well. The "Atmospheric Noise" of the corporate world faded, and my primary focus shifted exactly where it belonged—to planning more time with my children and actively participating in the grounding realities of their lives.

Reflecting on my past experiences—both my previous training business and these corporate endeavors—I recognized a clear pattern: I had spent years working grueling hours focused solely on other people's interests. This realization became my defining mandate: my next endeavor could not, and would not, demand that same sacrifice.

To ensure I honored this mandate, I dedicated myself to a period of deep reflection. For several months, my dreams were consumed by this process, offering a constant review of my thirty-seven years and the influential individuals who had shaped my course.

While this introspection reinforced the wisdom of my path, it yielded no practical indication of my next move—no surge of purpose, no immediate drive to proceed. As the moment of decision approached, I turned to my guides for a tangible sign. Their response remained an unwavering echo: I would simply know when the time was right. I had to once again endure the hardest lesson for a man of action: the strength of waiting.

CHAPTER VI

The Wasted Gift

The call to full capacity and the transition from "Doing" to "Leading"

The stillness of my deep reflection was suddenly broken by an email from an executive colleague. He reached out with news of a major construction project where the county agency was urgently seeking a highly specific professional: someone proficient in multiple engineering disciplines with a formidable background in safety. While he didn't yet have the official job description, he was so confident in my profile that he had already recommended me. He strongly urged me to meet with the project team.

Driven by a sudden spark of interest, I entered a high-stakes interview with the owner's representative, a seasoned veteran of the industry. For ninety grueling minutes, I faced a relentless barrage of technical questions spanning civil, mechanical, electrical, environmental, and safety engineering. I wasn't just reciting a résumé; I was defending a lifetime of integrated knowledge.

When his face finally registered approval, he provided the details of the scope of work. Though the role required a lengthy commute, the work schedule was the deciding factor—it aligned perfectly with my mandate to prioritize my family. The "Waiting" was over.

My responsibilities centered on interfacing with all key stakeholders—contractors, consultants, and agency personnel—across several ongoing construction initiatives. The contract was fixed at one year, culminating in a comprehensive report to the agency detailing my observations and proposed improvements. This defined timeline was the perfect strategic fit, providing the necessary window to revitalize my training business.

However, my first few weeks offered a jarring sense of déjà vu. I found myself once again surrounded by the same systemic failures—poor communication, coordination lapses, quality issues, safety breaches, and substance abuse—that I had faced on my first major site decades earlier.

Though it was difficult to witness these deficiencies, I understood my role was one of counsel, not enforcement. I offered guidance only where it was accepted, keeping my main priority clear: protecting my energy for my daughters' sports activities and ensuring our family time remained sacred.

During this contract period, the construction projects were marred by three tragic and avoidable fatalities—each a direct result of severely poor decisions and systemic neglect. As my tenure as the owner's consultant neared its end and I began compiling the final report, the agency's Construction Safety Manager approached me with a significant proposal.

He asked me to consider an ongoing, permanent position with the agency. With only several weeks left to finalize my findings and my plan to reboot my training business already in motion, I reached a crossroads. I agreed to consider his offer, promising a formal response while weighing the opportunity to change a broken system against my commitment to my family and my true calling.

Despite the gravity of the job offer and my looming decision, I saw no reason to alter my plans. My spiritual visits had been routine—until one night, in a profound sleep, my maternal grandmother materialized.

She looked exactly as she had at the cemetery, but her face was set in a fierce, angry scowl. She fixed her gaze on me and closed the distance, her left hand shooting out to grasp my right wrist with a vice-like, inescapable grip.

Suddenly, she drew a massive knife and violently severed my arm just below the elbow. "What are you doing?" I yelled in horror as the limb fell away. Her voice was firm, unyielding, and echoed with ancestral authority:

"Did you use every capability you possessed while you had it? Now that it is gone, do you regret not utilizing your full capacity? You have been given gifts; you must use them, or they are wasted."

As I watched her turn and depart, the urgent, jagged meaning of her message finally took hold. I awoke with a jolt, drenched in a cold sweat, the phantom pain of the loss still pulsing in my marrow.

The morning after the dream, I contacted the Construction Safety Manager to confirm my intention to apply. My focus had shifted to a singular mission: to utilize every capability I possessed for the safety of others. Because the work schedule aligned perfectly with my family mandate, I felt a powerful, integrated motivation to excel.

Upon joining the agency, I delivered my comprehensive final report. I was immediately struck by the leadership team's response; they didn't just file it away—they fully implemented every recommendation. This was a new professional reality. Unlike my previous corporate experiences, which often felt stagnant and lacked diversity in their upper tiers, this agency showcased strong ethnic diversity among its staff. This cultural breadth brought a fresh perspective to leadership, reinforcing my belief that I had finally found a system where my "Wasted Gift" could become a functional tool for change.

Adapting to the political atmosphere and the varying work pace of a county agency proved challenging. My years in private industry and with federal agencies—where protocols were stringent—had not fully prepared me for the complex web of local political concerns that shaped this agency's attitudes.

My initial assignment involved two major construction projects plagued by high injury rates and a staff that openly refused to adhere to state safety protocols. These contractors had been linked to two of the system's three recent fatalities. Having already witnessed management's failure to enforce change, I chose a simple, non-negotiable strategy: I immediately removed any worker from the project who refused to comply with safety requirements. This decisive action became my governing principle for every project that followed.

At thirty-nine, armed with the wisdom imparted by my guardians and my dreams, my working life fundamentally changed. I began to see and interact with everyone strictly as souls. Within this spiritual framework, human constructs like ethnicity, religion, and politics became irrelevant. I recognized that only younger souls rely on these concepts, often using them as a temporary crutch to navigate a world they don't yet understand. I was no longer an engineer managing employees; I was a soul navigating a field of other souls, some more practiced than others.

Despite this profound shift, my professional application remained clear: safety, like any motivation, is simply a matter of influence. In this human form, we are a species driven by emotions that can either enlighten or impair our decisions. To me, the true difference between an older or younger soul is the capacity to discern and act upon clear guidance. I chose to see the good in every soul I encountered, hoping to leave a positive influence on their path.

Reclaiming quality time with my children allowed me to share this philosophy directly. I implemented one-on-one soccer training and took them fishing at every opportunity—an activity that has always been my personal source of meditative comfort. I became an active force in their world, coaching my older daughter's team and founding my son's. These remain my fondest memories, all consistent with my primary mission: guarding them from negative influences.

However, maintaining this protective distance from the "Static" of the world weighed heavily on my parents, and the dynamics with my siblings grew strained. My father, ever strong-willed and assertive, continued to mandate his wisdom rather than offer it. I found myself caught between the ancestral respect I felt for him and the sovereign boundaries I had to maintain for the sake of my own children.

While I always maintained my own position, I never interfered in my father's dealings with my siblings; I did so out of respect for his role. I kept a close relationship only with my second-oldest and youngest sisters, as they had always been a positive influence. My oldest brother, however, was a different matter. He had finally returned to the United States and was in periodic contact with my parents, but my last visit with him two years earlier had been so unpleasant that I had deemed it our final encounter.

During a visit with my parents shortly thereafter, I immediately felt an intense, unstated uneasiness between them. The tension was palpable, vibrating in the silence. As I was leaving, my mother stopped me just outside the car, her voice hushed. She explained that my father was against her asking, but she felt compelled to speak: my oldest brother had called and asked them to contact me. He wanted to talk.

The moment I heard my mother's words, a clear message flashed in my mind: He is dying and wants to make amends. My mother admitted that my father had already refused the request, but she needed to hear my definitive answer. To verify the situation, I asked when she had last seen him and if he was alright. She calmly replied, "A week ago," confirming he appeared fine. But I knew the truth.

I fully understood that our paths would cross again in another role and another life—a belief I hold for any soul from whom I permanently distance myself. I confirmed my father's position and told my mother I had no interest in speaking with him. I simply did not have the heart to tell her what I already knew: that his time was short.

With an expression of profound relief, she smiled; she understood. Four months later, my brother passed away from lung cancer.

After the news, I braced myself, anticipating a visit from him in my dreams or as a spirit. My guardians, however, quickly intervened with a powerful assurance: while the influence our souls have on one another endures, the rules fundamentally change upon crossing over. Once a spirit returns home and the Life Review begins, they can no longer exert a negative influence on the living. Their ability to visit is strictly limited, granted only if they can convey a positive influence. I found immense comfort in this spiritual boundary, knowing his soul was finally on a path of growth.

This understanding marked a significant shift in my life and spiritual interactions. My constant dreams of being surrounded by my guardians' silhouettes ceased; their messages were now conveyed through an immediate, unmistakable emotional imprint, reinforced by an occasional voice.

Furthermore, the spirits that presented themselves to me no longer sought communication as they once had. Now, with simple eye contact, the moment they saw the expression on my face—realizing I was truly seeing them—they would simply leave, and I would continue on my way. I understood that not all the spirits I encountered had crossed over; these "uncrossed" spirits retained the ability to project negative vibrations and emotions as they drifted through the physical world.

This unique reality—this constant interaction with the unseen—is the essential context for the life I've chosen. These spiritual experiences have been both comforting and fulfilling, providing a clarity that the material world cannot offer. I have also realized that the discipline and boundaries I established early in my journey eliminated the need to seek out or accept traditional friendships—a decision made in my youth that I have fully embraced. My connection to the soul level is so complete that the social constructs of the "seen world" no longer hold a place in my requirements for a meaningful life.

My commitment to only interface with those who require my support and trust has clearly defined and protected my path. This boundary is not a wall, but a filter, ensuring my life force is directed where it is most needed.

Just as important is a pattern I have seen reinforced throughout my life: both young children and the elderly have always gravitated toward me. I view children as souls early in their journey—pure signals who deserve my absolute protection and support. I view the elderly as those who have endured the trials of a long and difficult path, thereby earning my deepest respect. They are the bookends of the human experience, and they are where I choose to focus my energy.

With this commitment in place, I treat all other interactions—whether professional or personal—that focus on petty, selfish, arrogant, or mulish issues as entirely irrelevant. They are merely the static of a world I have moved beyond, and they no longer have the power to alter my course.

Aside from my immediate family, I had previously met no one in my professional life who truly resonated with me. However, I finally encountered an old soul who had been part of a previous life. I had recognized him during my year as a consultant, though he worked for an affiliated company at the time. We never interacted until now, when he joined the agency directly and transitioned into a section within my department.

From our very first interaction, the comfort and trust between us were instant and mutual. An immediate, profound recognition washed over me: I remembered him vividly from a previous life during World War II. In that life, he was a younger American soldier—two years my junior—and we had forged a deep friendship in the brief time before his unit moved on. After several agonizing months, I encountered his unit again, only to find he had been lost in combat—a tragedy that had settled into the deepest recesses of my soul.

Today, the confirmation from my guardians is a great comfort, affirming that the strength of our bond remains a constant. It is a powerful reminder that while the road is long and the trials are many, the people we love are never truly lost; we simply wait for the next turn in the Latticework to find them again.

The constant validation of these deep connections only reinforced the reality I lived every day. It was a reality that shaped how I protected and guided my family, especially as my own spiritual experiences and abilities steadily intensified. I began to share these truths—with careful discernment—with my wife and children. I wanted them to understand the unseen architecture of our lives, ensuring they felt not only physically safe but spiritually anchored, guided by the same clarity that now dictated my every move.

The landscape of our lives changed profoundly when my second daughter, at the age of ten, began confiding that she was feeling presences and seeing spirits. I immediately emphasized the vital importance of open communication, assuring her that I understood these phenomena and could offer the guidance and context I once lacked.

My interest was matched by a deep-seated concern; I carefully monitored her emotional acceptance of these experiences and the potential intensity of her emerging abilities. Crucially, as her encounters increased, she showed no negative emotions or fear. Her ability to articulate the details was clear and remarkably consistent.

This consistency allowed us to delve deeper into the meaning of her experiences, especially as she began to describe feeling the internal states of others. Soon, she was picking up emotional impressions and the presence of spirits at the exact moment I did. It became undeniable: she was an empath, just like me. This shared, escalating ability became a powerful magnet, drawing us closer than I ever thought possible. Later in life, this mutual emotional transparency made it impossible to hide anything from one another; our connection was governed by the absolute honesty of the soul.

But this profound spiritual alignment was soon overshadowed. When my daughter was twelve, a visible physical change forced my wife and me to seek medical advice. The diagnosis was juvenile diabetes.

In that moment, I realized this was the activation of the directive my guardians had given me on the day of her birth. In recent years, they had made the milestones of her life clear—including the challenging course her health would take. Because of their warnings, I was not caught off guard; I was prepared.

Despite this new reality, watching our children succeed in their sports and sharing those milestones with my wife remained profoundly rewarding. These moments provided the emotional foundation we needed to face the trials ahead. That foundation was soon tested, not only by illness but by the passing of several extended family members, including my father-in-law, aunts, and uncles.

While these losses were difficult, they served to strengthen our core family bond. I was initially surprised by the scarcity of my own interactions with them after they crossed over; their appearances were brief, mere signals of presence. However, my daughters experienced a deeper, more frequent connection: their maternal grandfather often visited them, providing comfort and guidance within the sanctuary of their dreams.

This period was defined by the steady rhythm of family transitions: my oldest daughter graduated high school, my second was just beginning her high school journey, and my son entered junior high. At work, I remained diligent, focusing my attention on the projects and individuals where safety was a critical concern.

However, for the first time in years, I began to sense a new directive—a powerful impression to focus on individuals who had nothing to do with my technical safety remit. My guardians had long ago proven that there are no coincidences in the Latticework, and the sense of responsibility I felt for these specific people was undeniable.

While I recognized that this drive stemmed from deep past life connections, my guardians offered no specific reinforcement. They didn't need to; I simply knew I had to look after them. This impulse to guide was rooted in the same profound support that had shaped my own early career. The desire to pay forward the professional and moral wisdom I had once received felt less like a choice and more like a sacred obligation to honor the men who had once stood as my own sentries.

Realizing the complex web of events that brought our paths together was a masterclass in synchronicity; it reinforced my absolute belief that every soul we encounter and every intersection we experience is predestined—a necessary gear in the machinery of our collective journey.

This inner evolution, reinforced by the consistent presence of my guides, completely transformed my approach to others. Early in my career, I had been aggressively proactive, relentlessly driving my points home to preempt every possible mistake. I was a man who led through friction.

Now, informed by decades of experience, I could anticipate pitfalls long before they appeared. I learned the art of stepping back, offering patient guidance while allowing others the space to navigate their own adversity. This allowed them to internalize the lessons, even when they ultimately followed the path I had recommended. They were no longer just following orders; they were gaining wisdom.

I applied this same patient philosophy to my life at home. After years devoted to raising our children, my wife returned to the workforce to stay engaged. Our oldest daughter, now living on her own and preparing for marriage, remained a constant pillar of moral support. Our second daughter graduated and began her professional life, where she eventually met her future husband, while our son navigated high school.

Yet even as my life felt grounded and stable, this period was marked by several unexpected and jolting encounters. Our home, nestled in the high desert and guarded by mountains, was typically a sanctuary of comfort. This made the strange events that followed even more striking—a reminder that the "Latticework" never truly rests.

Even as life felt stable, the high desert sky began to reveal a new mystery. One evening, during my drive home, I stopped at a highway exit and felt an immediate, magnetic pull to look to my left. High above the mountain ridge, a small dot of aqua-green light appeared. It grew with terrifying speed as it crested the peaks—a clear indication of its immense velocity.

The object flew directly overhead, passing so quickly that it diminished and vanished into the night sky almost instantly. Shaken, I turned onto the back road and saw that I was not alone; several cars had already pulled over, their drivers stepping out to stare at the void in disbelief.

This proved to be only the first of many encounters over the following years. These events occurred across various locations and states, often growing more dramatic and revealing intricate details of the crafts. Over time, I began to feel their presence was intentionally directed toward me. This realization was complicated by moments of profound isolation: even when family or friends were present, I would see the craft clearly while they saw nothing. Eventually, I stopped asking. When I sought clarity from my guides, their response remained unwavering: No coincidences; it was intentional.

These experiences compelled a profound realization of the immensity of the universe and the true scale of our existence. They left me with a pervasive sense of our relative insignificance within the vast, cosmic machinery of our collective journeys.

Yet the prospect of intentional contact and the undeniable proof that we are not alone provided a necessary clarity. Witnessing events that demonstrate how far we have yet to advance successfully put everything into perspective. It served as a constant reminder that while our individual paths are vital, we are moving within a much larger, intentional design—an architecture of existence that extends far beyond the limits of our current understanding. I was no longer just a man in the high desert; I was a participant in a universal process.

CHAPTER VII

The Emotional Imprint

Interactions with the cosmic "Grays" and the value of human feeling

The period of raising our children was profoundly fulfilling, guiding us through a significant phase of our lives. That chapter expanded further when our oldest daughter married and gave birth to our first grandchild. We joyfully welcomed our son-in-law into the fold, viewing him as a young soul with an exciting journey of learning ahead. He was swiftly joined by our granddaughter—a wise, slightly older soul in comparison—who instantly enriched our existence. My daughter's established independence has always been a source of reassurance; we watched with pride as she began confidently navigating this new path of motherhood.

Following closely behind, our second daughter married. We embraced her partner as well—yet another young soul whose path is set for an advanced phase of learning. It is a source of deep comfort for my wife and me that both our daughters reside nearby, keeping our family "Latticework" tightly woven. Meanwhile, our son, having completed high school, has chosen to remain at home as he begins his career, keeping the heart of our family close.

As parents, we accept that raising children is a daunting responsibility, but for me, that duty is lifelong—it is a mandate that will exist until the moment I cross over. This understanding has been the bedrock of my life ever since I decided to start a family in my youth. Seeing my children thrive fills me with immense pride, yet it is accompanied by the bittersweet, sentimental "Imprint" of a father who knows just how quickly the seasons turn.

That sentiment surfaced in a vivid dream. In it, I had traveled back in time, watching over my oldest daughter when she was just four years old. I stepped away briefly to gather more toys, but when I returned, she was gone. A cold, absolute panic seized me.

I tore through the house and into the living room, where my wife and three children were gathered. I frantically begged them to help me find her, but as the words left my mouth, the surreal nature of the moment hit me with a jolt: the child I was searching for was standing right in front of me as an adult.

Heartbroken, the thought echoed through me: My little girl is gone. Immediately, my guardians intervened. Their message was clear and firm, reminding me that she—and every version of her—is never truly gone. In that moment, the linear constraints of time dissolved. I understood that the souls we love and the memories we treasure are permanent fixtures in the Latticework. This experience served as a powerful validation of my past-life dreams, reinforcing the proof that our souls—and our love—endure forever.

This capacity for change—moving beyond the constraints of past behavior—was beautifully illustrated by an experience that highlighted the profound growth we all undergo over time. When I was a child, one of my aunts, who struggled with poor health, was never warmly accepting of me. She always made her unwelcome feelings known whenever I played with my cousins.

Years later, after an era of distance, we finally crossed paths at a family reunion. With my daughters—then eight and four years old—by my side, I was astonished by her reaction. She was genuinely happy to see me and meet my family, expressing a warmth and acceptance I had never witnessed from her before. She had shifted her frequency.

Several years after that reunion, I was home alone late one night when I suddenly felt an unmistakable presence looming behind me. I turned quickly and was stunned to see her spirit standing there, smiling and gazing directly at me. An immediate thought formed in my mind: Why are you here? Without a word, she impressed a clear message upon my consciousness: "I wanted to see you." Then, she slowly faded away. Knowing instantly that she had crossed over, I waited in the silence. Moments later, the phone rang; it was my parents calling to confirm her passing. She had used her first moments of freedom to finalize the peace she had started at the reunion.

Losing my aunt was a difficult event that arrived during a broader period of family challenge and change. During this time, my parents retired. As their health declined, they remained resolute in how they wished to live out their final years. My two sisters and I made every effort to support them, and though we did not always agree with their decisions, we profoundly respected their right to make them.

I found it especially difficult to convey my appreciation to my father for all he had done for us. We both understood that my upbringing and my way of life in the United States were things he could not fully grasp; our internal languages were simply too different. My mother became the indispensable mediator, the bridge between our worlds. She would speak to us one-on-one, gently translating our intentions and helping us narrow the distance between our points of view.

As my father's health deteriorated, my sisters called, urging me to visit as soon as possible. I arrived for one final conversation the following morning, just before work. He began to reminisce about my youth, asking if I remembered the experiences that had meant so much to him. Seeing that he had accepted the end of his journey was near, I simply listened. I recognized the profound stage he was entering—the final acknowledgement of life we must all eventually face. He expressed deep concern about leaving my mother alone, and I reassured him that he need not worry. Hearing him speak without regret about his long journey gave me a great deal of comfort.

Two days later, while sitting with my wife and son, I suddenly felt my father's presence directly behind me. I spun around, fully expecting to see him, but I only felt his essence for a brief moment before it vanished. Then the phone rang; it was my niece, confirming that he had passed away.

After informing my family, I went into the backyard with my dog to collect myself. As I reflected on our last conversation, the weight of the loss began to surface. Suddenly, his voice spoke firmly into my right ear: "Don't cry. There is no need to cry. I am here and all right." I felt his attention turn toward my dog, and then, moved by an instinct I couldn't control, I let out his unique whistle—a sound I hadn't made since my childhood. It wasn't just a memory; it was a physical manifestation of his presence. He wasn't just "all right"; he was still a part of the very air I breathed.

For several weeks, his visits—manifesting through his voice and distinct emotional impressions—were constant. He let me know that he now fully understood my reactions to the decisions he had made involving my siblings, and he shared the underlying reasoning behind those choices. Some of those decisions, he admitted with newfound clarity, had been fueled by foolish pride.

Crucially, he wanted to confirm that he finally knew the depth of love and respect I had always held for him, just as I had always known the extent of his love for me. His presence, however, was noticeably refined, devoid of the abrasive characteristics that had defined him in life: his pride, his impatience, and his demanding demeanor.

Because I have always found a sanctuary in music—a passion he passed on to me—I eventually asked him for absolute proof that these visits were truly him. Immediately, an old Mexican song from the early sixties came on the radio—a song I used to sing to him as a child. Not only did I receive my proof in that moment, but I made the same confirmation request during every subsequent visit, and the result was always the same.

These experiences with my father gave me a deep, peaceful acceptance of the cycles inherent in our life journeys—a truth reinforced by my own guardians since childhood. I realized that death is not a wall, but a window that finally allows for perfect transparency.

Our personal drive and beliefs are profoundly, though briefly, influenced by the parents responsible for our upbringing. In our youth, they are our entire world, and we naturally adopt their traits. But as we grow older, we inevitably realize they are flawed humans, just like everyone else—a realization that allows us to establish our own distinct paths.

The critical lesson is this: the measure of acceptance—or non-acceptance—we show toward our parents as children is exactly what we will confront and experience as parents ourselves. It is a closed loop of understanding.

One year after my father's passing, we welcomed two new grandchildren. Our second daughter gave birth to our first grandson—an old soul with whom I immediately felt a strong, silent connection. Four months later, our oldest daughter gave birth to our second granddaughter. Just as I had with my own children, I instantly recognized this soul; I had known her in a previous life on this ongoing journey. Her spiritual gifts and abilities, however, are far more profound than my own empathic nature. I sensed early on that her reach would extend further than mine.

During this exciting time of new additions, our family "Latticework" stretched across the map; my second daughter and son-in-law accepted a new work endeavor that required a move to a rural area of Minnesota.

While it was difficult to see them leave, I was genuinely excited for my daughter and son-in-law to continue their path of growth. My wife and I made it a point to visit them twice a year, staying for two weeks at a time. I immediately fell in love with Minnesota; the old, spiritual energy was palpable–high, dense, and challenging. My daughter and I could feel the spirit energy vibrating almost everywhere we went.

We enjoyed getting to know their friends and exploring Minnesota and the neighboring states. Our travels always included stopping at any antique store we came across; for us, these were not merely shops, but repositories of human history where we could reliably sense the strong spiritual imprints left on the objects within.

On our third visit, we discovered an enormous barn that had been converted into an antique store. The space felt as vast as a hangar, partitioned by six-foot glass display cases filled with vintage items, with antique pieces covering the walls from floor to ceiling. When we entered, the only other person inside was the owner, who, like everyone we met in Minnesota, greeted us with a warmth that felt as genuine as the land itself.

As always, we immediately went our separate ways to explore the store. I began at one end of the barn, gradually working toward the opposite side where several old stagecoaches were displayed. While examining the items, I noticed a woman standing three sections to my left. Though three tall glass cases obscured her in detail, I could tell from her silhouette that she was neither my wife nor my daughter. When I finally reached the section where she had been standing, she was gone. Critically, there was no way for her to have left that area without passing directly by me.

As I continued toward the stagecoach exhibit, my daughter approached me rapidly, pushing my grandson in his stroller. Her face was tight with discomfort. As she walked past, she whispered a warning: "Don't go in there. There is a spirit that doesn't want us near."

My first instinct was one of immediate defiance; I was not going to let a spirit dictate my path or keep me from the stagecoaches. I proceeded anyway, but as I neared the first coach, an intense, heavy pressure began to build in my ears. The pressure intensified with every step until the world went silent—I could hear absolutely nothing.

While I didn't feel physically threatened as I had in past encounters, I recognized the boundary being set. I accepted that the entity was enforcing its own "No Trespassing" zone. I turned back and walked until the pressure completely subsided. I was standing there, recalibrating and preparing to try a different approach, when—seemingly out of nowhere—an older lady emerged from behind a stagecoach.

She was wearing an apron and had a dust rag slung over her shoulder, walking with purpose straight toward me. She stopped just five feet away, looked up at the wall directly behind me, and said, "I'm looking for a cuckoo clock and can't find it." Her voice was as clear as any I had heard. As she walked past me toward the far corner of the barn, I looked up at the wall where she had gazed. I saw several clocks—but no cuckoo clock.

I instantly turned to follow her with my eyes, but as she reached the corner, she vanished. Given that the corner was formed by two solid, windowless walls with nowhere to hide, I was stunned. I was utterly taken aback by how solid and real she had seemed; she didn't possess the translucent quality of a typical spirit. She moved with the weight and presence of the living, a resident of the barn's past still tending to her chores in the present.

I immediately realized this was the same woman I had briefly seen at the other end of the barn, leading to an urgent question: Was she trapped? Was she "uncrossed"? The answer returned as an immediate, clear impression:

When souls leave the living world, not all of them return "home" immediately. Those who remain—whether tethered by fear, anger, confusion, or lingering attachment—will linger in the gray, but they always find their way eventually. This profound confirmation provided me with deep validation, a final piece of the puzzle regarding the veracity of my lifelong spiritual experiences.

While I found clarity in the spiritual realm, the immediate concerns of my family soon demanded my full focus. We moved my mother in with my second-oldest sister as her health began to decline. My visits were often challenging; she visibly struggled to remain focused, the vibrant thread of our conversations beginning to fray.

As I listened to her, I couldn't help but remember the independent, outspoken woman she had always been. Her love and unwavering support were the architecture that made us who we are. Though she found my way of life in the United States difficult to grasp—much like my father—she was different in one crucial way: she always took the time to ask me about it. She reached across the gap of understanding, even when she couldn't see the other side.

It was during this period of her decline that the news arrived. As my wife and I were preparing to leave for a visit to Minnesota, my youngest sister called to tell us that our mother had passed away. Because her transition occurred just as we were set to depart, we made the decision to continue with our travel plans. I knew instinctively that her spirit was no longer tethered to her physical form, and indeed, I immediately felt her presence traveling with us.

She remained with us throughout the journey, though it wasn't until several weeks later, after I had returned to work, that she began to speak and leave clear impressions of her essence. Knowing that she—like my father—was now fully aware of our true feelings brought me immense comfort. The "Mediator" was finally at peace, seeing the truth without any need for translation.

Later that year, we returned to Minnesota for a Christmas visit. Immediately upon arriving, I sensed a sharp, quiet shift in the household's demeanor. Nothing was spoken, but the air was heavy with a deep, unmistakable tension. My daughter's disposition only confirmed my unease; the frequency of the home had changed.

Within a few months, they made the decision to move back to California, a move that led shortly thereafter to their divorce. Recognizing the weight of this milestone, I made sure they both knew the most important thing: they would always have our family's unwavering support. No matter how the external structures of their lives shifted, the foundation we had built remained indestructible.

After a two-year absence, we were happy to welcome my daughter and grandson back into our home as she continued her career. Simultaneously, we directed our focus toward supporting her ex-husband, recognizing that he would always remain an integral part of our extended family Latticework. This period of intense familial focus was soon interrupted by news from beyond our walls.

Several months later, my wife's mother passed away. Their relationship had been strained in recent years, and I focused entirely on providing my wife with absolute support. Throughout our time together, she had fought tirelessly to bridge the gap between her parents and me, standing firm against their prejudice toward minority groups. Her persistence had successfully won over my father-in-law, but it never fully softened the heart of my mother-in-law.

Following their passing, I would periodically receive visits from my father-in-law. He would convey messages of love for my wife and assure me of his deepening acceptance from the other side. Years later, when I was in my mid-sixties, my mother-in-law finally appeared to be present during one of his visits. Even then, the best I could receive from her were fleeting, ghostly impressions of understanding. It served as a sobering reminder that prejudice is a weight some souls carry long after the body is gone; it is a density that takes lifetimes to shed.

Despite the lingering weight of family history, my professional life offered its own urgent challenges. At work, I began initiating projects that required the formation of a dedicated safety staff reporting directly to me. Although I had no interest in the administrative burden of managing a permanent staff, I recognized this as a critical opportunity to formally unite the safety professionals I had been mentoring and developing over the years.

I viewed this as a vital extension of my role: an opportunity to take the "Safety Frequency" I had refined over decades and instill it into a team capable of guarding the perimeter with the same vigilance I had always practiced. I wasn't just building a department; I was creating a collective of watchers. Focused and eager to begin, I prepared to face the complex personnel challenges ahead with the confidence of a man who knew exactly how to stabilize a shifting environment—whether that environment was spiritual or corporate.

My wife's distraught call came while I was at work: my second daughter had been diagnosed with breast cancer. In that instant, every other priority vanished. My sole focus became supporting her and ensuring our family had the necessary strength to navigate this devastating diagnosis.

I have always lived to protect my family, believing all other pursuits irrelevant compared to their well-being. Now, I knew I was about to embark on the most painful and difficult journey of my life. The confidence I had built for personnel management was instantly repurposed and focused entirely on my daughter's care, beginning with the logistical urgency of scheduling treatments and locating the right specialists.

Though she undoubtedly sensed the initial fear of her mother, brother, and sister, my priority was to reinforce her own formidable strength. I wanted to act as a bedrock for her unwavering resolve as she took charge of her treatment decisions. Her courage never wavered—it was a profound, crystalline strength that I came to admire immensely.

The decision to undergo surgery provided an immediate, vital sense of hope. She maintained her focus on recovery with remarkable discipline, and with subsequent medical surveillance in place, she quickly returned to her professional life and a sense of normalcy.

For a time, my wife and I welcomed her and my grandson back into our home, allowing us to cherish the time we spent together as a family. It was a period of profound gratitude, a chance to reinforce our bonds under one roof. However, even with the return of this hard-won domestic peace, the world outside was growing increasingly unsettling. It was a quiet before a different kind of storm—a peace that would soon be tested by a reality that defied all earthly logic.

My sightings in the sky had increased dramatically in frequency, leading me to rely heavily on the guidance of my guardians during this tumultuous time. The intensity peaked one night when I was suddenly jolted from a deep sleep. My first thought was the television—which I often left on—so I sat up to see what was unfolding on the screen.

As I stared, a vertical split began to develop down the middle of the screen, like a curtain being pulled apart on a stage. A small hand pulled the split further, and a large head with a thin body shifted into view: a creature commonly known as a "Gray" was staring directly at me.

Its features were distinct: a massive head dominated by large, tear-shaped black eyes; small holes for ears; and an undersized, low-bridged nose. Its mouth was a mere slit, revealing small, thin lips. Amid my shock, I was immediately struck by a strange, undeniable sense of familiarity with the being.

He spoke instantly, his voice resonating directly within my mind without a single movement of his mouth: "I've been waiting for this. Come, let's go." Without hesitation, I rose and followed him through the shimmering split. We found ourselves standing in a vast, silent hallway. "Do you remember me?" he projected. "We were close friends. I have your favorite dish ready for you. Come."

Realizing I didn't need to speak aloud—that a mere thought was enough to communicate—I mentally asked, "Why are you doing this, and where are we going?" He replied that he was only taking a moment of my time to ask a few questions. They arrived in my mind instantly: "How does it feel to have emotions? Do you remember before?"

In that moment, the scale of my journey shifted. My struggles with my father's pride, the deep grief for my mother, and the terror of my daughter's illness were not just "human problems." They were the very experiences this being lacked. I realized that my capacity for emotion—the very thing that had made my journey so painful—was the "gift" the cosmic world was watching with such fascination. I was the transmitter for a frequency they could only study from a distance.

With this new understanding, I could feel him reaching into me, seeking to share and experience my emotions firsthand. Guided by his presence, we soon arrived at a vast room filled with beings of different sizes and shapes. It was clearly a dining hall, complete with tables where various entities were eating.

As we reached our table, I saw a bowl and several different shapes of eating utensils. He projected a sense of pride: "I made sure they prepared it the way you like it." I looked into the bowl and immediately recognized what appeared to be oxtail soup, a dish I genuinely enjoy.

I sat down, picked up a piece of the meat, and took a bite. Instantly, a bitter, profoundly unpleasant taste hit me—a flavor so wrong it felt like a chemical rejection. I quickly spit it out and mentally demanded, "What is this?"

He sensed my visceral displeasure but seemed confused by it. He simply projected one word: "Human."

The shock was total. It was a cold, paralyzing realization that hit me in my very marrow. I stood to leave immediately, the "familiarity" I had felt moments before vanishing. I realized then that his attempt at hospitality was based on a fundamental, terrifying misunderstanding of the human soul. To him, it was merely matter; to me, it was a violation of the sacred. A beat later, his voice returned to my mind, tinged with genuine bewilderment: "You don't like it?"

"No," I replied, my voice–mental and physical–hard with a resolve to leave. He was a creature of function; I was a creature of feeling. As we exited, he pressed further, relentlessly reaching into my mind to absorb the "confession" of my emotional memories. He was like a dry sponge seeking moisture, pulling the very essence of my history from me.

As we approached the door leading back to the hallway, he projected more questions about the mechanics of emotion. "This way," he announced, turning sharply in the opposite direction from our original path. As we proceeded down the long corridor, my emotional history began to pour out of me like a breached dam. He walked intently on my right, his head tilted back to stare up at me, absorbing every detail of the revelation as if he were witnessing the birth of a star.

We reached the end of the hallway and entered a dark, cavernous room. The moment we crossed the threshold, a dim light flickered on, revealing several control panels scattered across the space. He guided me toward one of these stations.

Taking his place on my right, he stood with his eyes unsettlingly level with my elbow, his gaze intense and unwavering. Suddenly, a massive projection erupted, filling three of the walls completely. The room vanished, replaced by the startling illusion that we were looking out through vast, clear windows into another reality.

The two walls to my right were utterly consumed by fields of stars, but the wall directly ahead displayed an enormous planet. Its surface was an incredible blend of pink, vivid blue, deep brown, and brilliant white—the most beautiful colors I had ever witnessed in a single celestial body.

I initially thought I was looking at Jupiter, but he abruptly projected, "Do you remember?" As I stared at the planet, the line between observation and memory blurred. I wasn't just looking at a projection; I was experiencing a deep, instructional "download"—a core truth about the functional entities that comprised this civilization.

Their life cycle is defined by purpose from the very first breath. Interaction with others is strictly forbidden until one is required to execute that function. Because no early social bonds are ever formed, the opportunity to develop emotions is eliminated, ensuring their existence remains purely functional. This mode of existence is not a flaw; it is an evolutionary path sustained over millions of years.

This universal diversity is vast: billions of planets host life at varying stages. Older civilizations are tasked with monitoring and supporting younger ones—a cosmic stewardship. This responsibility is complicated by the fact that each planet contains multiple interacting dimensions that continuously influence one another.

Furthermore, every inhabitant civilization is inherently limited by its planet's internal dynamics and its stage of societal development. Critically, the concept of time is only relevant within each planet's sphere; time does not exist in the universe at large. We all exist in a grand, simultaneous present, separated only by our frequency and our function.

As I stared intently at the swirling, multicolored planet, I felt his presence deep within me, relentlessly absorbing the imprint of my emotional memories. Suddenly, the vivid projection faded, my vision blurred, and the piercing sound of my alarm clock shattered the silence, yanking me back to my earthly life.

I bolted upright, my heart racing as I tried to dismiss the experience as a dream. Yet the evidence was undeniable: I felt the profound, bone-deep fatigue of a man who had been awake for twenty-four hours. More hauntingly, the peculiar, metallic, bitter taste of that "hospitality" clung to my tongue—a physical reminder of the gap between function and feeling that stayed with me for the rest of the day.

CHAPTER VIII

The Sacred Commitment

Fulfilling the vow to protect, the battle with cancer, and the journey home

Having always respected the cultures, religions, and struggles of other souls, I now find myself in a new state of mind. I have moved beyond mere tolerance to a much deeper appreciation for the wonderful beliefs different cultures bring to humanity, viewing our global diversity as a vital, integrated whole.

I have gained a newfound patience for souls challenged by selfishness, insecurity, and disrespect. I now recognize these attitudes not as inherent flaws, but as attributes heavily influenced by specific cultural contexts and evolutionary limitations. This perspective, born from recognizing these systemic constraints, has sharpened my focus on the unique nature of individual journeys.

I recognize the profound vulnerability young souls face as they navigate their paths, just as I observe older, more experienced souls actively working to prevent negative influences from distorting their decisions. My recent experiences—both earthly and cosmic—have allowed me to fully embrace this developmental process, regardless of the challenges it presents. This is a level of resolve I now strive to pass on to every soul I care for, acting as a steady frequency in a world of static.

While my focus remained anchored in family and work, the 2020 pandemic altered the world's routine, creating a global disruption of frequency. Many souls were lost, and while my family was fortunate to survive, the pandemic exacted a profound physical toll, striking me directly.

My physical condition deteriorated so severely that I genuinely believed I was reaching the end of my earthly journey. For twenty-four agonizing hours, I struggled to draw a single, full breath, forcing myself to remain intensely focused and awake despite a soul-crushing exhaustion. I was acutely aware of the overwhelming reality beyond my door—overcrowded hospitals packed with desperate patients—and the weight of that collective suffering was nearly unbearable.

Fearing I would alarm or expose my family to the virus, I held my ground in silence, protecting their peace until the very last moment. Just as I prepared to finally call out for help, a shift occurred. As abruptly as a light switch being flipped, my breathing returned to normal. The debilitating symptoms began to vanish as if they had never been there, leaving me alone in the sudden silence of a crisis averted.

I knew this dramatic recovery had a specific cause, and I immediately questioned my guardians. Their reply was swift and absolute: "You have not completed your task." They offered no further details, leaving me to face a world that was about to become even more demanding, but with the certainty that my presence was still required.

Tragically, in 2021, the pandemic claimed my brother-in-law. He was a soul who felt closer to me than a brother, a man I held incredibly dear. It took several months before he first visited my dreams, and a full year before he appeared to me in my waking hours, his frequency finally stabilizing enough to manifest.

His visits offered a profound assurance: he was "at home" with the others, watching over his family and my daughter, and continuing to support me on my journey from the other side. This validation was confirmed repeatedly, providing a spiritual anchor as our family continued to grow and shift.

The path he affirmed was soon underscored by joy when my son married and we warmly welcomed our daughter-in-law. Upon meeting her, I recognized her as a soul at a medium stage of her journey—a presence that resonated with a familiar, steady light and fit perfectly into our lives.

This joyous occasion served as a powerful reminder that the journey, though fraught with loss, is equally defined by new beginnings and deepening connections. Witnessing this ongoing growth has shifted my perspective, transforming the visceral challenges of the past into a more philosophical outlook as I look toward the future.

Our family grew once again with the birth of my son and daughter-in-law's child—our fourth grandchild and third granddaughter. As I had with her cousin before her, I immediately recognized the new arrival as an old soul, sensing an unmistakable connection that predated this lifetime. I also sensed that these two granddaughters are kindred spirits, bound by a shared frequency that will serve them well as they navigate their journeys together.

Seeking to understand the deeper purpose behind these constant moments of spiritual recognition, I asked my guardians for a sign of my own life-changing achievements. I expected a memory of my personal accolades or my own sports career; instead, I was surprised when the answer arrived with vivid clarity in a dream.

The memory took me back to my freshman year of high school. I had hoped to continue practicing with my junior high wrestling team, only to discover they had no coaching staff. The program was in limbo. After being sponsored by the high school coaches and approved by the district, I stepped up to lead the team myself. Every day, after finishing my own high school practice, I jogged across town to coach the junior high squad. That year, under my guidance, the team won the district championship.

The guardians were showing me that my "Task" has always been the same: to step into the void, to lead when there is no leader, and to ensure that those following behind me have the strength to win their own battles.

When I asked why this particular memory was chosen, the answer was instantaneous: The only truly important factor in our journeys is the impact we have on others.

While our youth is driven by the desire to overcome personal challenges, we eventually reach a point where those cherished touchstones of the past no longer hold the same significance. This revelation justified the shift in priorities common to the later stages of our journey. It confirmed why our concerns now center on meaningful interactions, and why the intense attachments of the past can finally be released. For me, the dream was proof that the spiritual guidance I have been receiving is consistent and that I am on the right path—the path of the steward, not the star.

This sense of spiritual alignment and renewed focus was critical for navigating the demanding realities I faced. While juggling my focus between family and work, I was also contending with my own private health challenges. Amidst this period, a bright spot emerged: our second daughter introduced us to her boyfriend. He possessed the unmistakable maturity of an old soul and was clearly her perfect match. We were immediately won over, accepting him into our family as we recognized the genuine love and dedication that bound them together.

Shortly after, they decided to move in together. It was a tremendous comfort to see their mutual dedication to my grandson and his seamless acceptance of their love. It was a relief to realize my daughter had finally found her true soulmate on this journey. Yet, even as I celebrated this peace, my focus shifted entirely toward them with a familiar, sharpening intuition. I instinctively sensed that our greatest challenges—and perhaps my final "Task"—were still ahead.

Soon after, the heart-wrenching news arrived: the cancer had returned with a devastating ferocity. The reality we had dreaded most was upon us, breaching the peace we had worked so hard to maintain. She immediately resumed the grueling cycle of chemotherapy and radiation, and doctors performed surgery to remove two tumors from her brain.

During those harrowing months, our family held strong, functioning as a single, unbreakable support system. We stood at the perimeter of her life, acting as a shield against the fear and uncertainty of the outside world while she focused every ounce of her being on the ordeal. She fought with a ferocity that matched the illness itself—a testament to a soul that refuses to be diminished by physical constraints.

My energy was constantly divided: I poured every ounce of my effort into reinforcing a positive frequency for my family and grandchildren, even as I wrestled with my own private anguish. This emotional juggling act was brutally difficult because I could physically sense my daughter's pain throughout her battle—a deep, resonant distress I had to suppress and hide from the rest of the family. Through our shared empathic bond, however, she was fully aware of the silent suffering I carried for her; we were two souls standing in the same fire.

During these months, the old, unsettling thought returned, a shadow from a more fearful time: Was this suffering a form of penitence? But recalling the stern, corrective guidance of my guardians, I dared not even ask. Instead, I wrestled with a different question: How many times must we endure these devastating cycles of pain?

The answer, when it came, was immediate and firm: Every soul chooses its own journey—whether for personal growth or to aid the evolution of others. It is a necessary process and, ultimately, a profound privilege, the true meaning of which can only be fully understood once we return to the Source.

This revelation was followed by months of increased spiritual activity. Family members who had passed on—my parents, my brother-in-law, and my father-in-law—began appearing with startling frequency, visiting me in both my dreams and my waking hours. They were no longer just memories; they were a presence, a growing assembly of watchers gathered for what was to come.

They were a steady source of reassurance, reinforcing the spiritual strength of our family and confirming that she was being looked after by those who had already crossed. This profound confirmation was more than a comfort; it gave me the anchorage and fortitude I needed to remain the steady "Yellow Light" for my family.

Later that year, the diagnosis was determined to be terminal. Her reaction to this devastating news was nothing short of inspirational to everyone around her; she did not crumble, but instead refined her focus. We both understood, without needing to speak, exactly what we now faced. It was a silent pact between two watchers.

For me, the most agonizing part remained the empathic weight of the pain consuming my family—especially my grandson. Yet, as we navigated her remaining treatments and the hollow halls of hospitals, our family's unity only deepened. We were no longer just relatives; we were a single, vibrating field of support.

Even amidst this challenging season, we celebrated my daughter's marriage to her soulmate with deep, defiant joy. He has been a pillar of strength and an essential part of our core since the moment they first met. Together, we stand as a unified front, focused entirely on the love that binds us—a frequency that no illness can diminish.

This truly special day—her wedding—offered me a rare moment to pause and thank my guardians and those beloved family members who have watched over us from the light. It was an opportunity to acknowledge the strength they provided—a fortitude that ultimately gave me the courage to fulfill the sacred commitment I received on the day of my daughter's birth. I had promised to guide her, and I would not falter now.

With that commitment fulfilled and time growing short, our conversations shifted toward providing context to our shared journeys. A lifetime of my past dreams and the steady guidance of my guardians suddenly snapped into perspective. I saw clearly that every disparate experience, every sighting, and every trial had been a long-term preparation for this specific moment.

Everything I could share to give meaning and understanding to my family became crucial; time was now of the essence. The visits and messages I received from the other side were immediately shared with my family and acted upon, ensuring that no guidance was left unheard. These talks during this sensitive, critical time were the most personally meaningful of my life. I acted as a messenger, relaying cherished words from our beloved family members who had passed, and offered my best answers to her deepest questions about what lay beyond the veil.

Eventually, her inquiries began to fade, yet I still had volumes of cosmic truth I yearned to share. However, a profound realization settled in: she was no longer relying solely on my words. She was now receiving that sacred communication directly, having established her own powerful, unmediated connection to the other side. She was becoming the light she was about to join.

Simultaneously, my focus was squarely on supporting every member of our circle, granting them the space to manage their emotions individually. I found myself repeatedly offering one piece of vital counsel: Avoid the mistake of setting expectations. While we naturally anticipate that others will react to tragedy as we do, I insisted that everyone must navigate their personal anguish in their own unique way to find the strength to move forward. There is no single "right" frequency for grief.

Though I struggled fiercely to maintain my composure, the empathic depth of her pain threatened to overwhelm me, pulling at my very foundation. In a moment of near collapse, I appealed to my guardians for unwavering direction. The response was instantaneous and sharp, cutting through my despair like a blade:

The appropriate time for your emotional release is yet to come; indulging those feelings now would be pure self-pity and unproductive.

This revelation acted as a sudden, perfect anchor. It wasn't a rebuke of my love, but a reminder of my function. It gave me the complete understanding I needed to stand fast, providing the steady, unwavering light my family required as the veil grew thin.

The guardians' response was underscored by powerful dreams that brought a cold clarity to my past experiences. I learned that in cases of a prolonged passing, our souls inherently know the departure date and begin a meticulous preparation for leaving this world—a mirror to the preparation made by the souls staying behind. This fundamental truth about the cycle of life was affirmed repeatedly by my parents and other guiding family members who watched from the other side.

They revealed that as we approach this final stage of our physical existence, we are naturally inclined toward a profound, graceful acceptance. It is not something we must fight to achieve; it is a frequency we simply step into. This realization—that acceptance is intrinsic to the soul's journey—gave me the spiritual armor needed to confront the stark reality of my circumstances.

As my own health continued to deteriorate and the physical demands of my work became a heavy burden, I leaned ever more heavily on the wisdom of my guardians. Crucially, the safety department I had established years ago now became an indispensable source of support, executing their responsibilities with the same precision and professionalism they had shown since day one. Seeing them stand on their own provided a different kind of peace. I realized then that a major career decision was inevitable and fast approaching: it was time to withdraw my energy from the world of industry to focus it entirely on the world of the soul.

The gravity of my career decision was entirely secondary to the profound challenges my family and I were facing. As my daughter's condition tragically worsened, the moment finally arrived. She crossed over and returned home, surrounded by the absolute love of family and friends. Her courageous and graceful departure delivered an enormous, final lesson for me, my wife, and our children: that a life is measured not by its length, but by the purity of its resonance.

I remain deeply proud and privileged to have been present for both her first breath and her final departure from this world. I knew, with a certainty that transcended grief, that she had beautifully accomplished every milestone set for her in this brief but meaningful life.

As I had on countless occasions throughout her life, I felt her presence envelop us in the room. I silently petitioned my spiritual guardians to assist her final transition, to smooth the path between dimensions. As I sat quietly in the crowded home, my gaze fixed on the ceiling, a vision unfolded before my mind's eye: I saw her walking confidently toward a chamber brimming with luminous silhouettes—her awaiting guardians and our family members who had gone before. She wasn't lost; she was being welcomed.

She had found her way home. A deep sense of relief and profound comfort settled over me, and I offered my final gratitude to the guides. The Sentry's watch, for this specific soul, was complete.

Late that same night, she appeared to me for the first time. Her message was decisive and urgent, bypassing the fog of my grief: "You must begin to look after yourself. You don't need to continue working; you have contributed enough to all of us. I will now remain with you and Mom, upholding the bond we all shared before our birth."

Since that initial visit, her presence has been a constant—manifesting reliably in both my dreams and my waking moments. She consistently reminds me of the rules governing the life review process, yet she never fails to assure me that she is overseeing and protecting the entire family. She has moved from being the one guarded to being the Great Guard herself.

Guided by the wisdom of my daughter and my guardians, I prioritized my health and heeded their advice to dedicate as much time as possible to my grandchildren and family. I left the professional world with immense solace. Since that ninth and final fatality early in my career, not a single life was lost on any of my projects. I take deep pride in knowing I made every effort to have a profound, positive, and productive influence on the lives of those I worked with. My earthly "Safety Mission" was complete.

My daughter's presence is now a permanent light, overseeing and protecting our family from her new, limitless vantage point. I am no longer watching the horizon alone; the "Sacred Commitment" has been fulfilled, and the Latticework remains strong. We are all, finally, home.

CHAPTER IX

The Spiritual Architecture of Family

Recognizing children as ancient companions and the contract of lineage

Having reached life's final vista, I pause and reflect on a lifetime of profound experiences that have spanned both the earthly and the cosmic. The guiding wisdom of my guardians and the deep, indelible lessons learned from every soul I have encountered—be they family, friend, or stranger—now come into sharp, singular focus. This final stage is not a fading away, but a sacred opportunity. It allows us to prepare for our afterlife review—a covenant made and a predestined milestone set before we ever embarked on this journey. It is the moment where the architect finally steps back to view the structure he has built.

Of all earthly influences, parents serve as the initial architects of our impressions; the legacy of their guidance—for better or for worse—persists as a blueprint throughout our lives. Our perspective on them evolves inevitably with age, as we begin to see the human being behind the parental mask. Personally, this understanding crystallized early: my father was the embodiment of respect for all, a pillar of transparent communication, and a living example of the necessity of defending one's core beliefs with integrity.

Looking back, I realize the space between us was not a flaw, but an accepted necessity in the grand design of this life. That distance taught me to appreciate—and eventually revere—the closeness I fostered in my own father-child relationships. We were bound by shared characteristics and parallel challenges, our lives echoing lessons from previous journeys across the stars. This profound connection eventually drew my spirit closer to his than physical proximity ever could.

The depth of his love and dedication to his family is a trait he successfully passed on to me, a torch handed from one Sentry to the next. Now, viewing his methods through the lens of my own experience, his approach to raising us has become far more understandable. I can clearly recognize his logic, regardless of how challenging or confusing it seemed at the time. Ultimately, he exemplified the truth all parents eventually realize: we strive to do the very best we can, utilizing every resource available in our frequency to protect and provide for the souls entrusted to our care.

My mother, matching my father's commitment, was equally dedicated to the structural integrity of our well-being. She maintained a strict, impartial balance, treating each of us without favoritism and requiring absolute respect—a standard that was never up for negotiation. I respected her deeply because her judgment was sound; her decisions, even in my father's absence, were resolute and absolute. She was, unequivocally, the essential bedrock that supported and guided our family throughout our formative years.

She, too, carried the wisdom of an old soul, navigating life's hurdles with a profound insight that felt ancient. My mother's unwavering kindness was expertly tempered by the strength of her stern discipline. In fact, when I misbehaved, I often sought out my father; I found his direct, physical punishment far less painful than facing the vibrational weight of her disappointment. Yet, despite her rigor, her unique laugh was a memorable delight—a distinct, resonant sound that offered a deep sense of security and comfort to everyone in the room.

What I cherish most is the memory of her evolving inner strength. Although she continually battled significant health issues, she met every obstacle with a profound acceptance and unwavering grace that I would later see reflected in my own daughter. Above all, her unreserved emotional sincerity became the anchor of our family bond during our youth. That vital quality—the courage to be emotionally present—remains a guiding principle I carry forward as a Sentry for my own lineage today.

However, even a deliberate architecture contains its trials. The lessons I learned from my five siblings—two brothers and three sisters—didn't just echo my past life experiences; they amplified them. As they focused on the grueling task of adjusting and settling into a new environment—the United States—I recognized that their process was distinctly different from mine.

Being older and more established in their ways, their adjustment required a greater degree of structural change. Crucially, their intense focus on this monumental transition—this survival of frequency in a foreign land—strained the development of a strong, unified family bond during that time.

I was taught early on that the strength of sibling connections is a direct echo of past life commitments. Our souls are drawn to resonate most deeply with those we have shared consistent and recent journeys with, entering into an agreement to further our collective growth in this lifetime. For siblings with whom a close bond does not materialize, or from whom we become distanced, the shared experience is understood as a lesson in individual sovereignty. We learn from their presence and witness their struggles, but we are ultimately tasked with navigating our own path, challenges, and decisions independently. We are separate stars in the same constellation, each burning with our own necessary light.

I will always cherish the memories of my siblings from our shared childhood. However, as we moved into adulthood and gained the freedom of independent choice, differences in judgment and intent inevitably surfaced, creating a rift in our collective resonance.

The emotional distance that developed between myself, my two older brothers, and my oldest sister ultimately reinforced the wisdom my guardians had shared: we are responsible for the integrity of our own light. By refusing to be pulled into negative influences, I maintained close, resonant bonds only with my two younger sisters, accepting the separation from the others as a necessary path toward my personal and spiritual goals.

This shift in my family landscape was a painful but vital lesson. It taught me to look far beyond the surface of blood relations to see the true nature of a soul. It was through this experience that I began to realize the truth of our eternal connections, leading me to view the family I eventually built not just as relatives, but as a carefully constructed sanctuary of shared purpose.

To understand the milestones of my children, one must first understand the partnership that made their arrival possible. My wife and I entered this life with a shared contract: to create a vessel of love and discipline that would allow these ancient souls to return and flourish. Our reunion in this lifetime was the resolution of a long and difficult history; my first and strongest impression of her was as my partner in ancient Greece, where I watched our life together cut short as I succumbed to illness, leaving a cycle unfinished.

This was only the first of many such echoes. I carried specific, vivid dreams of our lives crossing in various roles across the centuries, yet we never quite connected as partners. In one seventeenth-century journey, I was an English naval officer returning home with the desperate intent of marrying her, only to find she was already wed—a despair so heavy it led me to take my own life. Later, in 1920s Argentina, we were only days away from our wedding when I was killed in a tragic car accident while running a simple errand.

These echoes of "almost" made our eventual reunion in this life feel all the more destined. Now that we have finally found our timing, that destiny has manifested in the most beautiful way. With her steadfast love and unwavering support, I have found a profound resilience and the willingness to overcome even life's most daunting obstacles. The unique contrasts in our personalities and perspectives do not pull us apart; instead, they deepen our resonance, allowing us to balance one another in ways I never imagined. We have finally synchronized our signals.

She remains the grounding force in my life—a constant source of clarity that empowers us to reach our individual potential while harmonizing our strengths to achieve our shared family milestones. In the high-voltage moments of crisis, she is the anchor that prevents our circuit from breaking.

Our partnership provides the perfect balance between family cohesion and the freedom for individual growth. I truly believe that this journey was agreed upon by our souls long before this life began, setting us on a path where we can thrive together after centuries of "almost" connections. In this shared space, we honor our collective goals while nurturing the unique potential of every member of our home. We have built more than a family; we have built a sanctuary where ancient souls can finally finish their work.

I have come to see this family unit not as a biological coincidence, but as a deliberate Spiritual Architecture—a structure designed across lifetimes to support the mutual evolution of our souls. My children are not merely my descendants; they are ancient companions who have returned to walk beside me, each carrying a unique blueprint for growth that predates their first breath in this world.

By recognizing the roles they have played in the past, I am better able to support the milestones they seek to achieve in the present. The bond my oldest daughter and I share is forged by countless shared existences: we have stood side by side in battle, shared the embrace of family, and walked as friends and siblings across many previous journeys.

From the moment of her birth, I held a quiet, unshakable confidence in her ability to master the milestones set for her in this lifetime. This insight has brought me immense comfort; knowing our souls have already weathered centuries together relieved me of the heavy parental anxieties that often plague the modern mind. Because our frequencies are so much alike, she possesses a powerful independence and a sincere drive to achieve her goals while remaining deeply considerate of others. I watched as our mirrored characteristics played out in her life, and I saw her spiritual awakening mature with a beautiful clarity as she navigated the challenges of raising her own children—passing the "Instructional Memories" down to the next generation of our lineage.

Today, my eldest daughter is cultivating an inner harvest of acceptance and wisdom—the enduring legacy she will pass on to her own lineage. To impart this wisdom is the great milestone of her soul's current journey, and I have no doubt she will achieve it; her frequency is steady and her purpose is clear.

While I observe the unfolding purpose of my eldest, I recognize that a different, uniquely significant bond rested with my second daughter. She possessed the strongest immediate connection to me, having chosen to join me specifically for this high-stakes life journey—a clarity I felt from the moment she took her first breath. Knowing her soul from her previous life and understanding the difficult circumstances of her prior crossing, I accepted the challenges laid out for our mutual growth.

Our shared path would become one of the most important milestones of my own existence. Because of this deep resonance, I have felt the rhythm of her thoughts since her childhood; we operated on a shared frequency that required no words. As she matured, it became clear that her decisions—and even her deepest concerns—were perfectly synchronized with her spiritual purpose. In time, I realized she could feel the rhythm of my thoughts as well; we were two sentries guarding the same post.

Though we never spoke openly of this internal bond while she was here, she has confirmed it since her return to the Source. From her new vantage point, she validates many of my guardians' teachings, maintaining a line of communication that proves the Latticework remains unbroken.

This spiritual architecture extends to my son as well. Like his sisters, he and I share a bond forged over countless existences; my strongest impression of him is from a time when he served as my father, guiding me as I now guide him. Because of this ancient history, I have always felt a deep, innate certainty in his ability to navigate any adversity the physical world might present.

In this life, that seasoned foundation has manifested as an open heart and a genuine consideration for others—hallmarks that foster a deep, unshakable trust in all his relationships. Of my three children, he carries many of his mother's finest traits: that grounding clarity and emotional sincerity that have guided him so well on his path.

His milestones in this current journey are centered on the quiet, steady work of inner self-awareness and the expansion of acceptance. I know he will achieve these goals, just as he has in our previous journeys together across the stars. The wisdom he has gained—and continues to share—will leave a lasting, positive influence on his family for generations to come. There is a profound sense of pride and solace in knowing that this process of spiritual growth with my children does not end here. It will continue, evolving and deepening, long into our next journey together.

This spiritual architecture does not stop with my children; it blossoms further into the lives of my grandchildren. I recognize them not as "new" souls, but as seasoned spirits—the newest arrivals to our ancient circle—who have returned to gather the harvest of wisdom we have spent lifetimes refining. In their eyes, I see the continuation of our shared contract; they are the living proof that the love and discipline we poured into our family vessel will endure, echoing long after we have departed the physical realm.

Watching them, I realize that the growth we have achieved in this life provides the sturdy foundation upon which they will stand to reach their own unique milestones. They carry the torch of our lineage forward, ensuring that the light of our collective evolution never dims.

While our household forms the cornerstone of this spiritual architecture, the blueprint extends further still. Beyond the walls of our home, the echoes of our past lives ripple out into a wider web of kin—an extended family of souls who have played their own vital roles in our long and winding journey. These are the aunties, uncles, cousins, and elders whose lives have intersected with our own to provide contrast, support, and the necessary friction for our souls to sharpen. As I look toward this broader horizon from my final vista, I see that our story is woven into a much larger tapestry of ancestral purpose. We are a garrison of many, standing guard over a light that spans eternity.

CHAPTER X

The Ancestral Tapestry

Mirrors, roots, and the "Chosen Threads" of the extended family

If my immediate family is the sanctuary in which my soul finds its deepest rest, my extended lineage is the vast tapestry that provides its color and context. We often view our cousins, aunts, uncles, and elders as secondary characters in our personal drama—mere background noise to our daily lives. Yet, in the light of the impending afterlife review, we see them for what they truly are: a wide, deliberate assembly of souls who agreed, with great intentionality, to walk the periphery of our path.

This ancestral tapestry is woven with threads of shared karma and ancient promises. It stretches back far beyond our current memories to a time when our roles may have been entirely different, yet our underlying purpose was the same. We are a collective of travelers who have swapped masks and titles across the ages, all to ensure that the "Chosen Threads" of our lineage remain strong enough to hold the weight of our shared evolution.

To understand the strength of the tapestry, one must first look to the roots from which the threads emerged. Having been blessed with their physical presence, I experienced firsthand the weight and wisdom of my grandparents and elders. They were not merely characters in stories told by my parents, but living anchors who grounded our family in a profound sense of history and purpose. In the context of my soul's journey, I see them as the "Old Guard"—seasoned souls who took on the monumental task of establishing the karmic soil in which my parents, and eventually I, would be planted.

I have come to realize that many of the "predestined milestones" I faced were actually continuations of the work they began. We are a relay team across time; they ran their leg of the journey so that I could begin mine. Whether they provided a legacy of resilience or left behind knots of unresolved karma for us to untangle together, I view them with a deep, reverent gratitude. They were the first I knew to honor the contract of this lineage, and it is through their foundational strength that the rest of our ancestral web found the stability to expand into the light.

Extending from those ancestral roots are the aunts and uncles who served as the supporting pillars of my early landscape. In the grand design of our soul group, I see them as "alternative mirrors"—souls who shared the same foundational DNA as my parents, yet chose to manifest those traits through different lenses.

They provided the necessary contrast that allowed me to see my own parents with a more clinical, spiritual clarity. Through their lives, I witnessed the diverse ways our family's shared strengths and shadows could be expressed in the physical world. Whether they offered a sanctuary of kindness that softened my journey or the "necessary friction" of a challenging personality that forced me to sharpen my own boundaries, each played a vital role in my evolution. They were the teachers who showed me that while we are bound by blood and contract, we each retain the absolute sovereignty to interpret our roles in our own unique way. They proved that destiny is the framework, but character is the finish.

Walking parallel to my own journey are the cousins and in-laws—the soul peers who have shared the horizontal landscape of my life. My cousins are the keepers of our formative echoes; they are the spirits who breathed the same childhood air and navigated the same ancestral shadows, yet were tasked with entirely different missions. They are the mirrors of my own youth, showing me how the same roots can produce vastly different branches.

In-laws, however, represent a unique and sacred addition to the tapestry; they are the "chosen threads." While they do not share our ancestral blood, they have entered our circle through a deliberate, pre-incarnation soul contract. They bring with them entirely new colors and textures from their own unique lineages, enriching our shared environment. Their presence is often the source of the "productive friction" that sparks the most significant growth. They challenge our established rhythms and introduce new perspectives that prevent the spiritual architecture of our family from becoming too rigid. They are the bridge builders, connecting our ancient story to the wider world.

Finally, the tapestry finds its continued expression in my nieces and nephews—the newest growth upon the extended branches of our family tree. Watching them, I am struck by a profound sense of recognition; I see the familiar traits of my siblings being refined and reshaped within these younger souls. It is as if the family blueprint is being edited in real time, with each niece and nephew filtering ancestral strengths through the prism of their own unique spiritual purpose.

From my vantage point on this final vista, my role with them is one of a distant yet devoted observer. I am no longer the architect of their path, but a silent witness to their progress. I watch them navigate their own echoes with a quiet confidence, knowing that they are ancient companions tasked with carrying our shared wisdom into a future I will not physically see, yet will always spiritually inhabit.

As these emerging threads take their place in the weave, the full majesty of the Ancestral Tapestry becomes clear. Every role—from the oldest, deepest root to the newest, most fragile bud—has been essential to the integrity of the whole. When the time comes for my final review, I will look upon this vast, interconnected web not as a collection of coincidences, but as a masterpiece of spiritual collaboration. It is a testament to the enduring power of the souls who agreed, long ago in the light of the Source, to walk this magnificent journey together.

CHAPTER XI

The Completed Blueprint

A summary of a life lived with dual vision and spiritual resolve

I have lived my life as a guardian—sometimes of dogs, sometimes of men and women, but always, and most importantly, of my family. For decades, I moved through the physical world with one eye fixed on the seen and the other on the unseen, balancing the harsh, uncompromising realities of human industry with the delicate, high-frequency vibrations of the spirit realm. Today, that dual vision has merged into a singular, crystalline clarity. The watch is ending, and the blueprint is complete.

The milestones that once felt like insurmountable mountains have been crossed, and the "unmet goals" of those I loved have been beautifully realized in the lives of my children and grandchildren. I stand now not as a man burdened by the weight of duty, but as a soul enriched by the profound privilege of the journey. I see now that every "Yellow Light" of warning and every "Sacred Commitment" of love was a necessary stroke in the masterpiece of this incarnation.

Standing at the final vista of my journey, I find that the technical details of my career and the noise of my daily struggles have finally faded into the background. What remains is a clear, finished, and magnificent structure. I see now that I did not merely "live" this life; I was the site manager for a spiritual construction project planned with meticulous precision long before my first breath.

The blueprints were drafted in the light of the Source, and the materials were gathered across centuries of "almost" connections and ancient battles. My role was to hold the line, to guard the frequency, and to ensure the integrity of the build. To understand the blueprint of my soul—and to understand the resolve that carried me through the fire and the shadows—one must first understand the foundation upon which everything—my family, my career, and my very identity—was built: the Latticework.

I have always seen the world through a "dual vision"—perceiving not just the physical structures of engineering and industry, but a shimmering, multi-dimensional architecture that connects every soul and every event. On this grid, I have learned there are no coincidences.

Every person I encountered—from the "Ancient Companions" I recognized from past lives to the "necessary friction" of difficult siblings and colleagues—was a deliberate node in the weave. We are all liaisons of this structure, tasked with maintaining the integrity of our section of the grid with the same precision I applied to the safety of a construction site. By honoring our connections and recognizing the patterns of our past journeys, we ensure the strength of the collective tapestry.

Yet, I leave you with this final truth: this latticework is not merely a cold grid of geometry or a rigid blueprint of destiny. It is a living, breathing network, powered and given meaning by the pulse of the heart. It is love that lights the grid; it is sincerity that holds the threads; and it is our shared humanity that makes the architecture divine.

To the "functional" civilizations of the universe, emotion is often viewed as a contaminant that complicates purpose. But in the architecture of the human soul, I have discovered that emotion is the purpose. Through my encounters with the visitors from the stars, I realized that my mission was never just about logic or structural safety; it was about the profound privilege of feeling.

We are sent to this dense realm to learn how to carry the weight of the heart without breaking. Whether it was the "Warrior's Penance" of my youth or the "Deep Anguish" of my daughter's illness, I have learned that the depth of our suffering is the only true measure of the depth of our love. To feel the crushing weight of sorrow and the absolute warmth of joy is the highest form of spiritual achievement. This is the currency we carry home to the Source.

This currency of feeling became the fuel for my resolve—the driving force that allowed me to transform my empathy into a shield for those I served. In the hazardous world of heavy industry, "Zero Fatalities" was my professional gold standard. In my spiritual life, it was a sacred vow. To achieve "Zero Fatalities" in a world of friction, one must be unyielding. I used my sensitivity to anticipate pitfalls before they claimed a life, and I held that same shield over my home during our family's darkest hours.

I take immense pride in knowing that on my watch, the architecture held. I ensured that thousands of workers returned to their families, and I stood by my daughter until her final breath, ensuring her transition was not a fatality of spirit, but a triumphant return home. Now that the mission has been fulfilled and the tools have been set aside, the final stage of the blueprint awaits: the moment where the Architect reviews the work and finds that it is good.

Our journey ends not in judgment, but in absolute clarity. The Afterlife Review is the "covenant" we made before we arrived—the moment the scaffolding of the ego is stripped away, leaving only the pure resonance of our intentions. I have watched my father, my mother, and my daughter cross over, and I have seen the peace that comes when "foolish pride" is finally traded for eternal truth.

When I stand before the luminous silhouettes of my own guardians, I will not present a list of earthly titles or material wealth. I will present my record as a Guardian. I will show them a soul that refused to let its gifts go to waste, a heart that embraced the full, crushing weight of human emotion, and a blueprint that was executed with unwavering integrity.

The anger and the pain of this world are merely the scaffolding of the journey. When the building is finished and we finally return home, the scaffolding falls away, leaving only the "absolute, warm peace" of a soul that has fulfilled its contract.

I have seen the aqua-green lights in the desert sky, and I have felt the presence of ancestors in my hallway. I have protected the living and honored the dead. I am ready for my review.

The blueprint is complete.

THE GUARDIAN'S LEGACY

THE FOUR PILLARS

I. THE LATTICEWORK

Understand that you are never walking a random path. Every soul you meet and every challenge you face is a node on a shimmering, multidimensional grid. Your responsibility is to maintain the integrity of your section of the weave with honor and awareness.

II. THE WEIGHT OF EMOTION

Do not flee from the intensity of feeling. In the "functional" universe, emotion is a contaminant, but here, it is the currency of the soul. Carrying the weight of the heart without breaking is the highest form of spiritual achievement.

III. ZERO FATALITIES

In industry, it is a gold standard; in the spirit, it is a sacred vow. Use your sensitivity to anticipate the "Yellow Lights" of danger. Stand as a shield for those who cannot protect themselves, ensuring that no spirit is lost on your watch.

IV. THE AFTERLIFE REVIEW

Live your life for the moment the scaffolding falls away. When you stand before your guardians, you will not be judged by your wealth, but by the resonance of your intentions and the integrity with which you executed your blueprint.

READER'S GUIDE: DISCUSSION QUESTIONS

The following questions are designed to help you reflect on your own journey. Whether you are reading this alone or as part of a group, I invite you to use these prompts to explore the architecture of your own soul.

1. ON FOUNDATIONS

Javier compares the early stages of life to pouring a concrete foundation. Looking back at your own upbringing, what "materials" were used to build your foundation, and have they held up over time?

2. THE LATTICEWORK METAPHOR

A latticework is strong because of its intersections but open enough to let in light. How do you balance the need for "structural" discipline in your life with the need to stay open to new spiritual experiences?

3. INDUSTRIAL WISDOM

The author spent 40 years in heavy industry. Was there a specific "safety lesson" or industrial concept in the book that changed how you view your personal mental or emotional health?

4. THE CONCEPT OF "DRAFTING"

Javier speaks about "redrafting" his life's blueprint. If you were handed a pen and your life's blueprint today, what is one major structural change you would make to your current "spiritual architecture"?

5. RESILIENCE UNDER PRESSURE

In industry, materials are tested for their "yield point" (the point where they break). How has a period of high pressure in your life revealed your own yield point, and how did you reinforce yourself afterward?

6. LEGACY AND CONSTRUCTION

Javier founded The Latticework Press to create a lasting structure for stories. What is the "infrastructure" of the legacy you hope to leave behind for your family or community?

7. THE HIGH DESERT INFLUENCE

The environment of the High Desert plays a role in the book's atmosphere. How does your physical environment (where you live and work) influence your internal peace and spiritual clarity?

8. THE "INSPECTOR" ROLE

Javier spent years as a safety professional. If you were to perform a "safety inspection" on your current spiritual habits, what would be the biggest "violation" you'd find?

9. INTEGRATION

The book suggests that our professional lives and spiritual lives are not separate, but part of the same building. How can you better integrate your "daily grind" with your higher purpose?

10. THE UNFINISHED BUILDING

Every structure requires maintenance. What is one "renovation" project you are currently working on within your soul?

BEHIND THE SCENES

To understand the architecture of the soul, we must first understand the language of the builder. Here is the glossary of terms that formed the foundation of this work.

In the world of industry, words have precise, structural meanings. In the world of the spirit, these same words can help us understand how to build a life that lasts.

THE BLUEPRINT

The original divine intention for a soul's journey. While life often requires "Redlining" and "As-Built" adjustments, the Blueprint remains the steady reference point for our highest potential.

AS-BUILT

In construction, these are the drawings that show how the project was actually built, rather than how it was originally planned. In life, your "As-Built" is your true history—the honest record of your detours, mistakes, and triumphs.

FACTOR OF SAFETY

The capacity of a system to handle more than its expected load. A "Spiritual Factor of Safety" is the inner work we do (meditation, prayer, community) to ensure we don’t collapse when life delivers an unexpected weight.

FOUNDATION

The lowest load-bearing part of a building. A spiritual foundation is composed of your core non-negotiables—the truths you stand on when the ground around you begins to shift.

LATTICEWORK

A structure consisting of strips of material crossed and fastened together. To us, it represents the intersection of our human experiences and divine guidance—a structure that is incredibly strong yet open enough to let in the light.

LOAD-BEARING

A wall or beam that supports the weight of the entire structure. We all have load-bearing seasons; identifying what—or Who—is supporting you during those times is the key to resilience.

PLUMB

Being perfectly vertical. To be "Spiritually Plumb" is to be in total alignment with your higher purpose. If you are out of plumb, the structure may look fine on the outside, but the internal stress will eventually cause a crack.

REDLINE

Changes made to a blueprint during the building process. "Redlining your life" is the act of crossing out old, inherited beliefs and drawing in new, authentic ones that fit your current path.

STRUCTURAL INTEGRITY

The ability of an item to hold together under a load without breaking. It is the alignment of what you say, what you believe, and what you do.

ZERO FATALITIES

The ultimate goal in industrial safety. Spiritually, it is the commitment to "do no harm"—ensuring that our journey through this world protects the light in others rather than extinguishing it.

ABOUT THE AUTHOR

Javier Lora is a career safety professional specializing in heavy construction, hazardous waste remediation, and high-voltage energy systems, and the founder of The Latticework Press. With more than forty years of hands-on experience embedded in some of the most hazardous industrial environments in the country, he is widely known for an uncompromising commitment to "Zero Fatalities." Throughout his career, Javier has worked deep in the trenches of hazardous waste management, high-voltage energy, and critical infrastructure projects, guided by a singular focus on protection, integrity, and disciplined execution.

Beyond the hard hat and field reports, Javier is a lifelong student of spiritual architecture and a "Sovereign Soul" who has lived with a Dual Vision since childhood. His life has unfolded at the intersection of the functional world of engineering and the shimmering, multidimensional grid of the spirit realm, allowing him to navigate both with equal fluency.

A survivor of profound personal loss and a witness to extraordinary cosmic phenomena, he now dedicates his life to documenting the Latticework of soul connections, lineage, and spiritual responsibility. He resides in the High Desert of Southern California, where he remains a guardian of his family and a quiet liaison to the ancient companions who have walked beside him across lifetimes.

The Spiritual Architecture of a Soul is his first book.

ACKNOWLEDGEMENTS

I have spent forty years ensuring that structures are sound and people are safe. However, the architecture of this book was not built by my hands alone. It required the strength, friction, and guidance of a vast network of souls.

To the Master Architects: With profound gratitude and admiration to every soul—both the challenging and the helpful—who served as a necessary node in this journey. Whether through the "Necessary Friction" that forced me to grow or the quiet support that sustained me, thank you for reinforcing the structure of my life and guiding me toward the light.

To My Professional Kin: To my colleagues in the heavy industries of Southern California, thank you for the decades of grit and the shared commitment to "Zero Fatalities." You taught me that safety is a sacred duty, a lesson that became the cornerstone of my spiritual life.

To My Ancient Companions: To my children, thank you for accepting the contract to walk this density with me. You are the souls I recognized long before you arrived, and watching you build your own blueprints is my greatest joy.

To My Ancestors: To those whose "Chosen Threads" I weave into this tapestry—thank you for the roots. I hope this work serves as a worthy "As-Built" of the lineage we share.

Finally, to the Guardians who whisper from the yellow lights and the quiet echoes: The watch continues, and the foundation is secure.

ABOUT THE LATTICEWORK PRESS

The Latticework Press was founded on the principle that the most enduring structures are not built of steel and concrete, but of the stories we tell and the legacies we leave behind. Born from forty years of experience in heavy industry and safety, our mission is to provide a platform for "structural storytelling"—narratives that examine the frameworks of the human spirit, the integrity of our values, and the intricate connections that bind our past to our future.

We believe that every life has a blueprint, and every soul has an architecture worth exploring. The Latticework Press is dedicated to publishing works that offer both the strength of a foundation and the light of a new perspective.

If this journey resonated with you, join us on our website for deeper reflections and updates on our next project.

As an independent author and publisher, your voice is a vital part of the structure we are building. If this book helped you find alignment in your own journey, please consider leaving a review on Amazon. Your words are the bricks that help others find the path.

FINAL BENEDICTION

In the quiet space where memory meets the soul, may you find the strength of your ancestors and the clarity of your own divine spark. You are a chosen thread in an ancient tapestry, a warrior of peace in a world of noise. May the vow you have made to your own growth be your shield, and may the love you have gathered be your home. Walk in grace, build in truth, and remain steadfast in the sacred architecture of your spirit.

www.ingramcontent.com/pod-product-compliance
Lightning Source LLC
LaVergne TN
LVHW020635100826
845148LV00012B/2195

9798234062918